FORERUNNERS OF CHRIST

Forerunners of Christ

Studies of Old Testament Characters

by Joseph Fichtner, O.S.C.

THE BRUCE PUBLISHING COMPANY • Milwaukee

IMPRIMI POTEST:

BENNO MISCHKE, O.S.C.
Provincial, Province of Saint Odilia

NIHIL OBSTAT:

WILLIAM N. SCHUIT
Censor librorum

IMPRIMATUR:

✝ WILLIAM E. COUSINS
Archbishop of Milwaukee

December 22, 1964

To My Mother

Preface

ORIGINALLY the following narratives were attempts to acquaint myself with the main characters, major events, and majestic themes of the Old Testament. As a child many years ago I was introduced to the Bible by my teachers and the use of Dr. I. Schuster's *Illustrated Bible History*, but the years took their toll upon my memory. Since then the Bible was never an easy book to read. The modern biblical movement began and swept me along in its fervid stream. After reading in and about the Bible I was attracted by some of the key figures of the Old Testament and came to the idea that they would make likely subjects of conferences, and most of them were then employed in that way. More recently, after some more elaboration, they were written into articles and printed monthly in *The Catholic Home Messenger*.

The range of these essays is broad enough to include characters from three genera of writings found in the Old Testament — historical, prophetical, and wisdom literature. They may indeed seem too simple to some biblical scholars, but I really have no other apology to make than to admit how much material I borrowed from them, using it never too wrongly, I hope. We all have a huge debt of gratitude to pay to the men who spend a lifetime studying the Bible. Many of their findings and interpretations are included in these essays. Simple as the essays are, other readers may profit from them because of their very simplicity.

To select and treat Old Testament characters is not to isolate them from the social history and communal experience of Israel. Sacred history, as well as secular history, revolves about central figures. The characters presented here had an important part to play in unfolding the plan of God for His people. God normally dealt with His people through leaders.

This, then, is a gallery of portraits of key personalities in the Old Testament who recapitulate and give direction to their era. They incarnate the ascending movement of faith and mark the stages of this gigantic catechumenate of the world which is the Old Testament. Seen in their own milieu, time, social and religious context, they initiate us personally into the Bible and God's plan as it is revealed therein. All of them, excepting perhaps the last, provide the background and preparation for the New Testament.

In one of his many inspiring lectures on the Bible, the prophetlike Father Barnabas M. Ahern, C.P., pointed out how many Old Testament characters are models of virtue. "Their God is our God; their human nature is our human nature." The grace of Christ, which is one, found its way into their lives too. I share this conviction with him. God speaks to us in the Old Testament through its great leaders and their message still has relevancy for us.

Men and women of the Old Testament, no less than men and women today, taught and portrayed virtue and vice. Their characters were outstanding not because they never failed God, never sinned against His will or plan of life for them, but because by success or failure they were instrumental in shaping the course of salvation-history. God operated through them whether they were unfaithful or faithful to Him.

To my confreres, who no doubt see in me reflections of the characters I try to describe, my sincere thanks for their merciful charity.

JOSEPH FICHTNER, O.S.C.

Crosier House of Studies
Fort Wayne, Indiana

Contents

Preface vii

I Our Father Abraham . . . 1

II I Am Your Brother Joseph . . 10

III Moses, the Man of God . . . 19

IV Joshua, the Valiant Leader . . 30

V Ruth the Moabite 39

VI King Saul 46

VII David the Beloved 55

VIII Elijah the Tishbite . . . 65

IX Isaiah, Greatest of the Prophets . . 75

X Judith, the Heroic Jewess . . 83

XI The Confessions of Jeremiah . . 91

XII   Ezekiel in Exile   100

XIII   A Dialogue With Job   .   .   .   109

XIV   Daniel, His Dreams and Visions .   .   118

XV   John the Baptist   128

FORERUNNERS OF CHRIST

Our Father Abraham

In my mental image of him, Abraham stands head and shoulders above all other characters of the Old Testament. He is more prominent than Noah who precedes him and Moses who follows. Beginning with Chapter 11 of Genesis, we read that Abraham was so stalwart a believer in God's promises, so ready to do God's bidding, so faithful in observing the one religion and the one worship, that God was spoken of as the God of Abraham. God assumed this title to Himself later when He appeared to Isaac and Jacob. God let it be known to Moses that the Israelite religion did not originate with him. It began with Abraham, and it has been continued, developed, and fulfilled in the Christian religion we profess and practice today. Our Christian background is Hebrew. As Pius XI remarked, "Spiritually we are all Semites," for we are all spiritual descendants of Abraham.

Time and Setting

Chronologically, Abraham takes us far back in human history, almost too far back for historians to inform us exactly as to the time he lived. The educated guess nowadays is that he lived about the year 1700 B.C. We are living in the second millennium after Christ, so we can say, using round figures,

that Abraham lived about the same time before Christ as
we live after Him. Yet Christ could say today, as He did
at the midpoint of this sweep of history, "Before Abraham
came to be, I am" (Mt 8:58).

Reading the story of Abraham, however, doesn't leave us
the impression that he was so ancient. One of the great
personalities of all history, he reflects the foils and foibles
of men of destiny. God would have His plan of salvation —
His covenant or personal relationship with mankind — fulfilled in Abraham, a leader of the people of God. Much the
same human material God employs now as He used then.
Yet today the name of Abraham is recalled with honor by
all the monotheistic religions — Judaism, Christianity, and
Islam, comprising almost half of the world's population.

The two great civilizations of Abraham's day were Egypt
and Babylonia, and Abraham was a native of the latter. The
Bible introduces us to him when he was a grown man, one
of three sons, already married to a woman named Sarah.
He was settled in South Babylonia, in the Chaldean city of
Ur (a barren place in modern Iraq). Babylonia was a fair,
rather rich stretch of country lying in between the Tigris and
Euphrates rivers, forming the eastern tip of what has come
to be called in geography the Fertile Crescent. The Fertile
Crescent, you will remember, is that long, half-moon-shaped
piece of land that is known in the Near East for its fertility.
In Abraham's day, South Babylonia was enjoying a high level
of civilization, with well-populated cities, with art, law, culture, and politics. In Ur, Abraham and his wife had a secure
and comfortable living, the kind that people hate to give up.
When a homesteader has a good tract of land, he will hate
to leave it or be driven from it. So it was with Abraham.
To say the least, he was well situated.

Abraham was a patriarch, a father-ruler comparable to the
men we know nowadays who by loving, supporting, and
ruling their families mirror in their lives the Fatherhood of

God. History reveals that patriarchs inhabited tents and wandered about, grazing their herds and flocks. Abraham was a seminomad sheik. He may have stayed long enough in one spot to grow some grain; the rest of the time he tended his sheep and oxen. It was at this stage of his life that the call came from Yahweh to Abraham to leave this well-settled and well-civilized people, the Chaldees, and start the trek toward a foreign land. "Leave your country, your kinsfolk and your father's house, for the land which I will show you; I will make a great nation of you . . . in you shall all the nations of the earth be blessed" (Gen 12:1–3).

The Call of Grace

This moment of history sets in relief the grace of God. Abraham experienced the same call of grace which every one of us has felt in his Christian vocation. God's choice fell upon Abraham, and the divine grace addressed itself to him. This vocation embodied the entire religious mission of the people of Israel. Abraham was chosen by God, "selected out of grace," as St. Paul says (Rom 11:5). No doubt, it was a matter of free choice, manifesting Yahweh's initiative. Looking at such an election retrospectively, the Hebrew writer named "Yahwist" attributed it to God: "Indeed I have chosen him" (Gen 18:19). But when we seek out the motive for this gratuitous preference, we discover no other than love: "For love of your fathers he chose their descendants . . ." (Deut 4:37). The freedom of that loving choice is brought home to us forcefully by Isaiah: "Look to Abraham, your father . . . when he was but one I called him" (Is 51:2). The choice was made without any merit or claim on Abraham's part.

Since his people were worshipers of many pagan gods, particularly a moon god called Nanna, Abraham must have found it hard to be uprooted from them. Abraham had wide possessions; he was a man of substance and influence within his community. Now he was asked to leave all this and to start afresh. On the surface it wasn't a very attractive offer. Yet Abraham chose to accept it because he had faith in God.

It was the first of three major separations Abraham was to undergo in his lifetime. At God's call, he took his wife and nephew Lot, packed up his belongings, and went to the strange, unknown land of Canaan or Palestine. God promised him that he would be the father of a great race, and He kept repeating that promise as a sort of refrain. So his pioneering spirit led Abraham to Canaan, which history has described as a land "flowing with milk and honey." Yet it was hilly and unfruitful in parts, a rugged land promising threats as well as blessings. Canaan was nonetheless fitted providentially to be the home of a great nation, the crossroads of the ancient world, lying as it did between the two big empires of Babylonia and Egypt, and in the path of the later civilizations of Greece and Rome.

The heartrending separation took place. Abraham and his family traveled northwest to Haran (south of Armenia and near Asia Minor). Along the way he was fed by the promise that his was to be a chosen nation, a chosen people, the people of Yahweh. Together they were to have and to preserve the religion and worship of the One God. The caravan moved onward to Shechem. In Canaan, time and again Abraham set up altars of stone to the Lord and sacrificed to Him. The second stage of his journey was over; he had come the distance from Ur to Shechem, roughly eight hundred to nine hundred miles.

A Man of Faith

Under the influence of the call of grace, Abraham responded by faith and obedience, both of which led to his justification. "Abraham believed the Lord, who credited the act to him as justice" (Gen 15:6). That in short is the story of his success. There can be no mistake about it, because

St. Paul has analyzed it further and written of it under inspiration. Because of his faith, Abraham became "the father of all who believe" (Rom 4:11). His faith in the one and all-powerful and merciful God mingled with a deep and lasting trust. As St. Paul has phrased it, "Abraham hoping against hope believed, so that he became the father of many nations" (Rom 4:18). He was "fully aware that whatever God has promised he is able to perform" (Rom 4:21). His success story is repeated in every Christian life that is filled with belief and trust. Daily duties and events are but sign-posts pointing out to the Christian the plan of salvation.

For a while life must have looked rosy to Abraham. Then came the second decisive episode in his life. Famine struck the country of Canaan, compelling Abraham and his wife and Lot to drift southward to Egypt. For a while they had been out of pagan surroundings, now they were back in them. Abraham now showed himself to be faltering in his faith. He was willing to gamble away his wife to save his own skin. His wife, Genesis tells us, was "a woman beautiful to behold" (12:11). Her beauty was rumored to Pharaoh, who asked Abraham to have her. Abraham on this occasion proved to be fickle and fearful of his life. He pretended that Sarah was his sister (actually she was his half sister), fearing that if he told Pharaoh that she was his wife, the ruler would take his life in return for hers. But Yahweh was not deceived. He had sanctified that marriage and intended to keep it holy. Pharaoh was notified by Yahweh in a series of great calamities that he would have to hand Sarah back to Abraham un-harmed. The Pharaoh rebuked Abraham for his sly trick and sent him hustling to Canaan.

Canaan, the Land of Promise

When we meet Abraham again, in a third episode, he is back in Canaan and enjoying life once again, for in the meantime the famine has left the land and his herds and

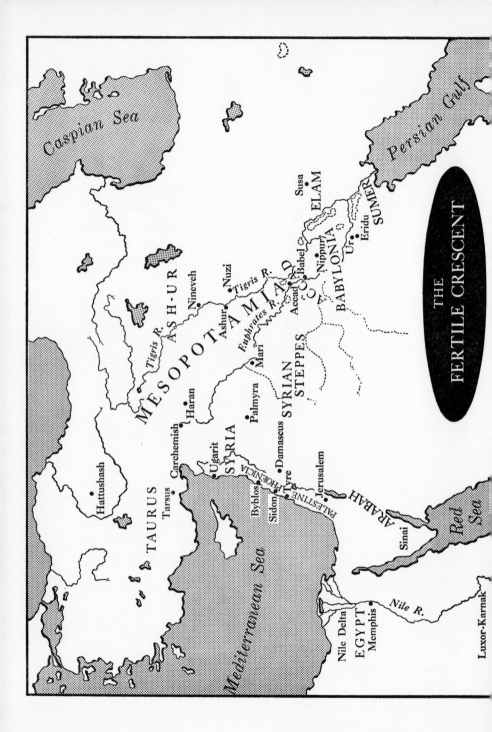

THE FERTILE CRESCENT

flocks have increased and multiplied. Abraham is rich; he has plenty of gold and silver. And his nephew Lot's condition has bettered too. He has herds and flocks and a camp of his own. When the shepherds of the two camps begin to quarrel among themselves, their masters have to make a heartbreaking decision. A second separation breaks into Abraham's life. The two, Abraham and Lot, have each to go his own way. Good, generous, and magnanimous as Abraham is, he allows Lot to take his pick. Lot decides in favor of the Jordan district and settles at Sodom, the first of that infamous twin-city combination of Sodom and Gomorrah.

Abraham and Lot, however, did see each other again, for Abraham came to Lot's rescue later. He gathered together a fighting company of 318 men, plus a smaller contingent, and fought off an Elamite king and other eastern kings who were terrorizing and ravaging the countryside about the Jordan. Lot was saved, and the spoils taken by the enemy were returned to him.

On his return Abraham met the non-Hebrew king and priest Melchizedek. The finer details of their meeting are related by the author of the epistle to the Hebrews (7:1-3). Parentage and genealogy of Melchizedek are left a mystery by Scripture, but the lineage of his priesthood is traced through Christ to all priests. "Thou art a priest forever, according to the order of Melchizedek" (Heb 7:17).

Old as Abraham was, Yahweh continued to tell him that his progeny would be as many as the stars of heaven, that his race would be numberless. Whatever faith Abraham had in Yahweh's word, it did not convince Sarah. When she was told that in her old age she would bear a son, she laughed, but God had the last laugh. She finally did bear a son who was named Isaac. According to the divine command, to seal the covenant between Yahweh and Abraham, the child was circumcised on the eighth day after birth. Circumcision initiated him into the people of God. To abide by this command, Christ too was circumcised on the eighth day.

Although the Lord saw the family love of Abraham and Sarah, he wanted to put Abraham to a supreme test. He called for a separation that Abraham must never have anticipated. As a seminomad, it was a sacrifice of faith and obedience to transfer from one country to another. But as the father of Isaac it was asking much of him to sacrifice his own son. That was exactly what Yahweh demanded of Abraham, and Abraham immediately complied. He was about to plunge a knife into the boy's back, as they stood on a mountaintop, when an angel of the Lord stayed his hand. God only wanted to put Abraham to a test, nothing more. He would not have him offer human sacrifice such as the pagan peoples around about him did. He would have him prefigure the willingness of God the Father to offer up His only Son for the salvation of mankind. Then and there, in the name of the Lord, the angel promised even greater blessings to Abraham, repeating that his progeny would outnumber the sands of the seashore.

Obedience, the Work of Faith

Abraham's obedience is no less remarkable than his faith. Is it not obedience which produces good works, the spontaneous expression of faith? In fact, Genesis highlights Abraham's obedience more than his faith. "Walk in my presence and be perfect," was Yahweh's demand upon His patriarch. And the father-ruler did not hesitate or flinch or argue. "In your descendants all the nations of the earth shall be blessed, because you have obeyed me" (Gen 22:18). This example of obedience was recalled to the son Isaac (cf. Gen 26:5).

Moreover, a special blessing was to befall Abraham's race: "In you shall all the nations of the earth be blessed" (Gen 12:3). What that special blessing was only we Christians have come to know through the call of faith. The Messiah-

Lord was born of the race of Abraham. But the outstanding fact of Abraham's life is not that the Messiah was carnally descendant from him. Our Lord saw more importance in the relationship to Abraham by faith than by carnal descent. He called Zacchaeus, a sinner, a son of Abraham because of his belief. The capital thing in our Lord's estimation is that we practice the virtues of the father-ruler — faith and obedience. The Hebrews who surrounded our Lord and kept clamoring that they were the children of Abraham, were told bluntly: "If you are the children of Abraham, do the works of Abraham" (Jn 8:39).

We often meet up with Abraham, this simple, pastoral man, daily in the liturgy. His name appears in the *Magnificat* and *Benedictus* canticles, and in the missal along with Abel and Melchizedek. The Epistle of the Thirteenth Sunday after Pentecost affords us the opportunity to recall his life and virtue. If we are "of the faith of Abraham, who is the father of us all" (Rom 4:16–17), his spirit and example will help us to penetrate into the pagan society around us, and we will be able to live and hand down the faith to future generations. His mission in life is no different from ours today, "for he was looking for the city that has the foundations, of which city the architect and the builder is God" (Heb 11:10).

I Am Your Brother Joseph

"Go to Joseph." How often have you not seen that adage carved in stone or printed? Do you recall offhand its origin? We usually refer it to St. Joseph, the husband of Mary and the foster father of Christ. Upon investigation, however, we find out that "Go to Joseph" was an ancient byword which we have Christianized. It was spoken of an earlier Joseph, perhaps the first Joseph known in recorded history. As a byword it introduces us to the original Joseph's life story.

The story of Joseph is acknowledged to be "one of the most beautiful in all literature." Like all literary masterpieces, it should be read in the original, for the story is bound to suffer in any retelling. And that is why the whole story will not be repeated here, but enough of it will be retold, in three episodes, to help whet the appetite to read it in the Book of Genesis. So, for spiritual reading, I would recommend that you open your family Bible to the first book, then turn to Chapter 30, verses 22–24, where the story begins. You will then have to skip to Chapter 37, read all of it, and flip the pages to Chapter 39, where you can continue the story to the end. Chapters 30, 37, 39, and following will tell you that unforgettable, patriarchal story of Joseph, a man of sterling character, a man all of us can imitate. He was surely one of the saints of the Old Testament.

Hebrew storytellers often reflected upon the life of Joseph and saw the hand of Yahweh in it. The unknown author of the Book of Wisdom, writing about a hundred years before Christ, suggests a synopsis for his story:

> She [divine wisdom] went down with him into the dungeon,
>   and did not desert him in his bonds,
> Until she brought him the scepter of royalty
>   and authority over his oppressors,
> Showed those who had defamed him false,
>   and gave him eternal glory (10:14).

The Canaan Youth

The first episode of Joseph's life takes place in Canaan, the Near East land where God had led Abraham, his wife, and nephew Lot to begin the Hebrew nation, the people of God. Joseph was one of twelve sons, the firstborn of the famous Rachel, Jacob's wife. Jacob had been named "Israel" by God, because he was the strong man of God from whom God's people were to be descended. His twelve sons were to found the Israelite nation or kingdom, just as Christ was to found the kingdom of His Church upon the twelve Apostles. Joseph was the great-grandson of Abraham himself. Abraham, Isaac, Jacob, Joseph — that is how the family lineage runs, or at least that is how it is handed down to us in the Bible.

We first take special notice of Joseph when he was a lad of seventeen, a Hebrew teen-ager, his father's favorite son "because he was born in his old age" (Gen 37:3). The fact that he was a favorite son must have been unmistakably evident to his eleven brothers. It aroused them to jealousy, and their jealousy grew into hatred, so that they "could not even greet him" (Gen 37:4). They had some reasons for disliking him, for he had a little of the upstart in him. One

reason was that he had witnessed a crime of theirs, possibly
it was lustful conduct, and turning informer he told his
father about it. And they were jealous because Jacob had
shown favoritism by giving Joseph a multicolored, ankle-
length garment or tunic customarily worn by the sons of
kings.

Joseph piqued them too with his fanciful dreams. In his
dreams he kept appearing as a ruler over his mother and
brothers. He was a dreamer of dreams, or so they nicknamed
him. His dreams pictured them to be like sheaves of grain
that bowed down to him, and like eleven stars that worshiped
him. The loving father tried but failed to erase the bad
impression his son made on his brothers.

Finally, in their jealousy, they plotted to take revenge on
him. It all happened the day that Jacob sent Joseph in search
of them and he tracked them down pasturing flocks near
Dothan, about forty miles north of Jerusalem. They would
have killed him and thrown his body into an old dry cistern
if Reuben, the oldest brother, had not interceded for him.
He persuaded them to cast him alive into the pit, intending
to rescue and deliver him later to his father. But once Reuben
was out of sight, they decided to sell him as a slave, for
twenty pieces of silver (the legal price), to Arabian mer-
chants who were on their way to Egypt. Imagine, for the
price of a young male slave, they got rid of their brother.
Afterward they used a subterfuge to deceive their father;
they brought home to Jacob his son's garment reddened with
goat blood. The father was stricken with sorrow. The boy
had been killed by wild beasts.

The Egyptian Slave

So much for the Canaan episode of Joseph's life. The
scene changes. His story continues in Egypt. It has a strong
Egyptian flavor to it and is faithful to Egyptian custom and
life, from which we can conclude that it was written by

someone well acquainted with Egypt. We must conjure up
the sight of the Nile and its delta. We must pass from the
simple, patriarchal world of flocks and herds to the life of
cities and palaces, from the deserts and hills of Canaan to
the sophisticated streets of Egypt. Egypt was a prosperous,
fertile land at times when the Nile irrigated the soil.

The ruling dynasty in Egypt at the time of Joseph's arrival
was very probably the Asiatic Hyksos, who swept down to
conquer Egypt and rule it from 1720 to 1550 b.c., give or
take a decade or two. You can well imagine that the native
Egyptians did not relish the rule of foreigners, and in Egyptian history this period of Hyksos government was considered an age of decadence. The Hyksos rule, however, helps
historians to set the date of Joseph's life — about 1600 b.c.
The Hyksos introduced the horse-drawn chariot, turned Egypt
from a peace- and home-loving people into a military and
foreign-minded nation. They often hired non-Egyptians to
help them control the country. That fact has to be remembered in order to understand how Joseph was able to rise
so high in officialdom. Joseph was, like the Hyksos, a Semite,
and this kinship no doubt was of help in his successful rise.

Once in Egypt, he was sold to Potiphar, the captain of the
royal guard. The captain came to like Joseph and to trust
him with his household affairs. The character of the young
man, together with the ever present, provident care that
Yahweh had for him, helped him to prosper and triumph
in this foreign land.

Time passed by. Then a woman entered into his life —
none other than Potiphar's wife. Joseph began to feel the
tug of Egyptian worldliness at his sleeve. She was a woman
spoiled by rich, beautiful living, luxurious and licentious.

Youthful and handsome, Joseph was repeatedly tempted
by the lady of the house. Chaste character that he was, he
must have recognized that he was associated with people
who loved pleasure and had scant appreciation of the malice

of sin. Was he to do in Egypt as the Egyptians did? The woman's conduct agreed with what scholars have learned about ancient Egypt; women at that time were not models of morality but often gave in easily to vice. But the woman was not to have her way with him. When she found out that he spurned her advances, she accused him before her husband of solicitation to adultery. Potiphar put him in prison. But cast into either a pit or a prison, Joseph providentially emerged and scored even greater triumphs.

The Merciful Deliverer

Events then telescope into a third episodic period in his life. In Canaan Joseph was called a dreamer of dreams; in Egypt he came to be known as an interpreter of dreams. During his two-year sojourn in prison he successfully interpreted the dreams of the Pharaoh's butler and baker, both of whom had been imprisoned, possibly, for conspiracy or treason. When the Pharaoh himself began to dream strange dreams (Egyptians put entirely too much stock in dreams and magic), Joseph was called in to divine seven years of plenty and seven years of famine ahead. Then he proved himself once more by prudently and capably advising the Pharaoh how to run his department of agriculture. Clean-shaven, perfumed, clad in a white, pleated garment, as the Egyptian custom dictated to anyone who appeared before the Pharaoh, Joseph was appointed second in command — an Asiatic favorite of an Asiatic sovereign. This is how he became the prime minister or viceroy of Egypt.

Everything he predicted came true. The fifth of the produce of wheat, corn, and other grain, which was stored in granaries all over the empire, was more than enough to tide the Egyptians over the years of scarcity. As soon as they felt the pangs of hunger, they went running to the Pharaoh for food. "Go to Joseph," he advised them, "and do what he tells you" (Gen 41:55). As the famine spread far and wide beyond the Egyptian borders, the rumor traveled with it, "Go to Joseph." To all who came to him Joseph sold wheat for cold cash or in exchange for flocks and lands. In this way all the Egyptian land but that in the hands of the priestly caste became government-owned. Neighboring countries bought supplies, and among them were the Canaanites, and among the Canaanites were Joseph's brothers.

Seven years of bumper crops and two lean years passed by before Joseph's brothers felt the pinch of necessity and came to purchase grain. Joseph put them through a series of tests, not to revenge himself, nor to deceive them, but to teach them how much their former deception had cost them. First he accused them of spying (Egypt had to protect her eastern borders) then of stealing (Joseph had hidden a silver cup in Benjamin's grain sack). And each time he dealt with his brothers, he demanded a hostage. Finally his courage left him, and dismissing his attendants he tearfully revealed himself to his eleven brothers, "I am Joseph." They were struck dumb in his presence, so that he had to repeat himself, "I am your brother Joseph, whom you sold into Egypt. Do not be distressed nor angry with yourselves that you sold me here. . . . God sent me before you to preserve a remnant for you in the land, and to deliver you in a striking way" (Gen 45:4-5, 7).

Joseph's last request to his brothers was to fetch his aged father Jacob. After a twenty-year separation, what an affectionate family reunion they had! With five more years of famine still to come, Joseph picked out a district about 40 miles northeast of present-day Cairo called Goshen, where Jacob and his sons, their wives, children, and many dependents, symbolically seventy in all, could settle and live unmolested by the Egyptians. But Jacob would not leave his native land before consulting with Yahweh and learning His will. Then in a vision to Jacob, Yahweh echoed His promise to Abraham, "I am God, the God of your father. Do not fear to go down to Egypt, for there I will make you a great people" (Gen 46:3).

At this stage of sacred history, the citified Egyptians were not concerned about their seminomad neighbors, for the simple reason that they looked down upon seminomadic life. In the meanwhile Egypt fitted into God's plan for His people. Egypt was a friendly power under whose aegis the people of God could live, prosper, and multiply. Thus Jacob's patriarchal family formed the nucleus of a nation. They entered into a new world with new opportunities. Had they remained in Canaan, they would apparently not have grown into a great nation. In the way that Yahweh saw fit, the patriarch Joseph was instrumental in accomplishing Yahweh's will for His people.

After Jacob's death, Joseph continued to treat his brothers with kindness. He made them promise that they would bury him as they did their father Jacob, in Palestine. Seeing that his own days were numbered, he left them a last will and testament that, if interpreted spiritually, betokens a fitting climax to every human life: "I am about to die, but God will certainly come to you and lead you up from this land to the land which he promised on oath to Abraham, Isaac and Jacob" (Gen 50:24). When he died, his body was embalmed, Egyptian fashion. What the book of Sirach has to say about him might serve as an appropriate epitaph on his tomb: "Was ever a man born like Joseph? Even his dead body was provided for" (49:15).

We have noted only the bare essentials of his life story. But why note them at all? Because, as St. Paul explains, though speaking about another situation in the life of the people of God, "these things came to pass as examples to us," "all these things happened to them as a type, and they were written for our correction" (1 Cor 10:6, 11). In the speech he gave to the Hebrews before he was stoned to death,

St. Stephen briefly narrates the history of Joseph among other bits of history, and concludes, "As your fathers did, so you do also" (Acts 7:51). He seems to draw a comparison between Joseph's life and that of Jesus. So I think we are justified in asserting that Joseph was a type of Christ. He prefigured Jesus the Savior.

Joseph and Jesus

What correspondence can we see between Joseph and Jesus? In the first episode we witnessed the eleven brothers green with jealousy and black with hatred. The same evil motivation drove the contemporaries of Christ, blood brothers of His, to kill Him. "He came unto his own, and his own received him not" (Jn 1:11). Like Joseph, Jesus was gifted with a prophetic spirit, and yet He was not "acceptable in his own country" (Lk 4:24). It was only after Joseph was moved out of his homeland that his real talent and worth were recognized. Jesus shook Nazareth dust off His feet because it was questionable whether any good could come out of Nazareth.

The second episode revealed Joseph struggling against worldly enticement. A weakhearted, less-principled man, finding himself in a land and among people where he could live and act incognito, would not have given a second thought to pleasing a woman at the price of a mortal sin. Jesus associated and ate with sinners but was Himself sinless.

The last scene of our story presents the people of God safely settled in the land of Goshen. Joseph had merited a blessing for them by his suffering and ill treatment. Both Joseph and Jesus passed through suffering to glory, both saw a day of terrible humiliation, both met with exaltation, both were rewarded for forgiving their trespassers. To summarize their lives, one would have to say in a word that theirs is a story of forgiveness.

The Character of Joseph

Reading the life story of Joseph puts us in contact with a great and lovable character — candid, honest, chaste, religious, magnanimous and forgiving, loving, businesslike. A beautiful character, a model of perfection.

I use the word "character" purposely to draw attention to the value of good character and the need of early home training. Human character, especially in childhood and youth, is pliable and flexible; it can be shaped and groomed. Grace, which is the life of God, was meant to work along with character and not supplant or subsidize it. God ordinarily does not send us His grace like a bolt out of the blue. He cautiously fits grace to character. Between the two — grace and character — there is a silent but strong interplay.

God's lofty designs are meant for men of character. In the patriarch Joseph we have an example of a man of character whom God used for His own designs, in spite of so many human attempts to frustrate them. Joseph himself recognized divine designs in his life and told his brothers so, "You intended evil against me, but God intended it for good" (Gen 50:20). Joseph's dreams of greatness did not make him great. His character was tested, and like gold that is tested in the fire, the testing made him great.

Moses, the Man of God

WHEN we last heard of the people of God, the Israelites, they were in Egypt, in the northeast corner called the land of Goshen. This land had been assigned to them by the Hyksos Pharaoh, through the intercession of Joseph. Jacob and his family had settled there. For a long time — 430 years according to one tradition — the Israelites remained in Egypt and prospered. But the last hundred years were unhappy for them. The Hyksos kings who had been so tolerant and generous to their fellow Semite, Joseph, and his people, had been replaced by native Egyptian Pharaohs "who knew nothing of Joseph" (Ex 1:8). One Pharaoh after another saw the Israelites grow in numbers and wealth; Egypt began to have a problem of overpopulation. Numbers of them had to leave the crowded Goshen corner and mingle with the Egyptians in their cities.

In the thirteenth century before Christ, the Pharaohs began to fear them and oppress them. They did not want to be rid of their colonists entirely; they found them useful enough for agriculture and architecture and craftsmanship. They merely wanted to keep them in their place, in a condition of inferiority and state of slavery. The Israelites were put to hard labor, building the supply cities of Pithom and Raamses on the northeast Egyptian border. They had to manufacture bricks, to supply the straw for the bricks. The Pharaohs thought that if they were kept at slave labor, they would die early and rear small families. When this protective measure did not work, the Pharaoh gave orders that the midwives should strangle every Israelite male child. That did not work either. Finally the royal decree came that every male child born of Israelite parents should be drowned.

In the Court of Pharaoh

Such was the sad condition of the Israelites at the time of Moses' birth. Moses was to be drowned. Though his parents lived close to the royal palace, his mother was able to circumvent the decree and successfully hide the child for three months. But she could not keep the child concealed much longer. She then had her daughter Miriam take the child to an offshoot of the Nile River, place him in a pitch-coated basket in the midst of some rushes. There he was found providentially by the Pharaoh's daughter. When she looked for someone to nurse him, she was tricked by Miriam into taking Moses' own mother. What a lasting influence that mother had upon her son! How she endeared him to his people becomes evident in the rest of our story.

Moses grew up in court surroundings and, according to St. Stephen who tells his story, "was instructed in all the wisdom of the Egyptians" (Acts 7:22). He was given all the scientific and military training available. This knowledge would come handy for him later, when he was to be called by God to lead the people out of Egypt. All the while that Moses was at court, and this was for forty years, he felt a close kinship with his people and sympathized with them. One day when he saw one of his countrymen mistreated by an Egyptian foreman, he angrily killed the man on the spot and buried his body in the sand. News of the killing eventually reached the Pharaoh, probably Raamses II, who determined to take revenge upon Moses. This was the providential incident which compelled Moses to flee to the Midianites, to learn a shepherd's life and habits there, to find solitude for meditation, and to take a wife from among Jethro's daughters. Leaving the land of his birth, he perhaps relinquished forever the opportunity of gaining great power in the service of the Pharaoh.

The Encounter With Yahweh

We have arrived at a point of his life when God took a direct hand in it, when he entered into an I-thou relationship with him. One day as Moses was watching his father-in-law's flock near Mt. Horeb (or Mt. Sinai according to another Hebrew tradition), he saw a thornbush aflame in front of him, but the bush did not burn. Out of the bush came the sound of a voice calling him, "Moses! Moses!" God introduced Himself as the God of Abraham, Isaac, and Jacob. He asked Moses to lead His people out of Egypt. "But Moses said to God, 'Who am I that I should go to Pharaoh and lead the Israelites out of Egypt?'" (Ex 3:11.) Moses feared taking the assignment because he felt himself incapable and because he was slow and stuttering of speech, far from the good public speaker that would draw and command a crowd.

His spirit was bolstered when God told him not once but repeatedly, "I will be with you" (Ex 3:12). The last strains of that refrain still ring in our ears because it was spoken again by Christ to His apostolic Church, "Behold, I am with you all days, even unto the consummation of the world" (Mt 28:20). What a wealth of meaning lies in that original promise of Yahweh's! It reveals a great future ahead — the personal presence of God not only with Moses but with His people of all ages.

Even after God gave Moses Aaron, his brother, for a spokesman, and turned his shepherd's staff into a miracle-working instrument, Moses wanted further assurance. He had to have some credentials to present to the people, so he asked God who He was. Unless he were given a name, he would be unable to convince his fellow Hebrews of the religious experience he had on the mount. The Hebrew language has handed down to us that mysterious though awesome name, Yahweh. "I am who am" (Ex 3:14). Various interpretations have been given to it ("I am he who causes to be," "I am he who is always there"), yet all of them leave the name shrouded in mystery, as it should be. God is inexpressible. He is the wholly Other, one who transcends us infinitely, whom we cannot fully grasp with our thoughts.

At any rate, for God to reveal His identity was a very intimate act, which a prophet like Hosea was to compare with the intimacy between husband and wife. God left His name for the first time for a memorial to all generations. His Hebrew name, as was customarily thought among the Israelites, was synonymous with His personality. It helped to identify Him, a sort of seal or signature expressive of His character.

And still Moses was reluctant to take up his mission, to assume leadership. God then worked two miracles to reassure him: He turned Moses' staff into a serpent and changed the color of his hand to albino white — leprous as snow.

Moses Before Pharaoh

Finally, with Aaron for a spokesman, Moses with his wife and children set out to liberate the Israelites from the Egyptian yoke. The record shows that his life of leadership was filled with one disappointment after another, but he stood his ground, never compromising. At first he had to contend with the recalcitrant Pharaoh, who one minute was willing to let the people go and the next minute changed his mind. Moses had to keep referring to God for help against this vacillating Pharaoh. By means of his miraculous staff he was able to send plague after plague upon the Egyptians: bloody water, frogs, flies, boils, hail, and, last and worst of all, the killing of all the firstborn Egyptian children and beasts. Moses kept shouting into the Pharaoh's ear the word God had spoken to him, "Let my people go" (Ex 5:1).

Ten plagues in all. Unbelievers try to explain away the ten plagues, saying that they were merely natural blights, like the river turning red from pollution by fungi, plants, and insects. Such natural phenomena, it is true, did happen in Egypt, but not in the way the Bible reports them. They were told because in the eyes of Israelite faith they were wonderful and significant, expressing God's presence and activity among His people. They were predicted by Moses. They began and ended as he wanted them. They were more intense than all others. They were destined by God to show His power and might, to show who was the real God, and to force the Egyptians to let His people go. Even the Egyptian magicians who tried to perform similar marvels and duplicated two of them, had to confess defeat in the end, admitting that "This is the finger of God" (Ex 8:15).

The last plague was contemporaneous with an event that is memorable in Old and New Testament history. God instituted at this moment the feast of the lamb and unleavened bread which His people were to keep in memory of their deliverance out of Egypt. Moses conveyed God's orders to the people: to identify their homes they were to smear the lamb's blood on doorposts and lintels. "Seeing the blood, I will pass over you; thus, when I strike the land of Egypt, no destructive blow will come upon you" (Ex 12:13). The event and the memorial meal have ever since been called the Pasch or Passover. "When your children ask you, 'What does this rite of yours mean?' you shall reply, 'This is the Passover sacrifice of the Lord, who passed over the houses of the Israelites in Egypt, when he struck down the Egyptians, he spared our houses'" (Ex 12:26–27). Each year on

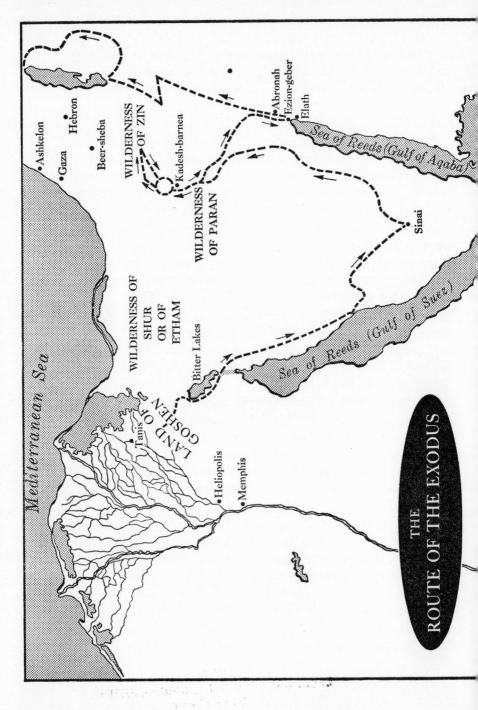

THE
ROUTE OF THE EXODUS

Mediterranean Sea

Ashkelon
Gaza
Hebron
Beer-sheba

WILDERNESS OF ZIN
Kadesh-barnea

WILDERNESS OF PARAN

Abronah
Ezion-geber
Elath

Sea of Reeds (Gulf of Aqaba)

Sinai

WILDERNESS OF SHUR OR OF ETHAM

Bitter Lakes

Sea of Reeds (Gulf of Suez)

LAND OF GOSHEN

Tanis

Heliopolis
Memphis

Good Friday we read the account of it in the second scriptural lesson, followed by the many references to it in the Gospel of St. John.

The Exodus From Egypt

The final stage of the great exodus from Egypt took place at the Red Sea (rather "Reed Sea" because of the papyrus reeds growing on its borders). We see Moses leading the Israelites, about 600,000 plus women and children, according to the biblical figure, though students of the Bible think the figure is exaggerated. The Egyptians were in hot pursuit of them with 600 chariots and 1000 horsemen. They would have caught up with the Israelites if God had not worked the strange miracle of blowing aside the waves, probably somewhere along the stretch where the Suez Canal now lies. The Israelites escaped at night while the Egyptians were drowned as the east wind ceased blowing and the waves once again came together. The watery walls joined and engulfed the Egyptians but not their Pharaoh. The Israelites were out of reach.

Moses' leadership was partially successful. God kept His promise to His people. Their crossing the Red Sea unmolested was an event that would always be recounted in memory of their Yahweh. "Sing to the Lord, for he is gloriously triumphant; horse and chariot he has cast into the sea" (Ex 15:21). As long as Moses their leader was with them, they knew that Yahweh was in their midst. The exodus would forever be a central event in Israel's memory, a symbol telling future generations of Israelites of God's plan for His people, of His readiness to watch over and assist them. It is the subject matter of that enchanting canticle, the *Exultet*, which is sung on Holy Saturday.

Beyond the Red Sea lay the desert. We must not imagine a long and wide empty plain, a wasteland. It was rather a land spotted with oases where the Israelites could graze their flocks. The oases of the Sinai peninsula, which is shaped like a triangle, were enough for several thousand people but not for the 600,000 and more that the Bible speaks of. On their march through the desert, Yahweh was with His people once again, guiding them alternately in a pillar of fire by night and a pillar of cloud by day. And yet His people could not keep content. "Is the Lord in our midst or not?" (Ex 17:7.) They were hungry and complained to Moses. They forgot their terrible lot in Egypt and longed again for the fleshpots of Egypt. Moses interceded for them. God sent them an abundance of quail to eat. He rained down the sweet-tasting, honey-like manna. They were thirsty. Moses struck the rock with his staff and water poured forth. God called them a stiff-necked people.

On Mt. Sinai

The Israelites wandered southward and encamped at the foot of the triple-peaked Sinai range. The place is very memorable in sacred history, for there Moses underwent a unique religious experience. On Mt. Sinai God knew and spoke to Moses "face to face, as one man speaks to another" (Ex 33:11). Moses stayed atop the mount for 40 days. From God he received the Torah, the tablets of the Ten Commandments.

The commandments were given to Moses against the background of darkness and light. God revealed Himself under the phenomena of lightning and thunder, darkness and cloud, which symbolized His presence among His people. The Ten Commandments were part of the covenant, the religious I-thou treaty into which God entered with His people. He was to be their God, and they were to be His people. The covenant did not in any way lower God in their estimation. It meant that He would be loyal to them if they were loyal to Him, faithful to His promises and ready to help them if they kept their end of the bargain. "For I, the Lord, am your God; and you shall make and keep yourselves holy, because I am holy" (Lev 11:44). They were called upon to worship Him alone and keep His law: "You shall be to me a kingdom of priests, a holy nation" (Ex 19:6).

Moses was not so meek when, on his return from the mount, he found his people worshiping a golden bull (the bull was a symbol of divinity). Terribly angry, he smashed the stone tablets and made the Israelites grind the bull to ashes and eat them. Then he returned to the mount and received a second copy of the Ten Commandments.

In Sight of Canaan

The rest of Moses' story is unessential to our purpose. What we have related can be read in more detail in the Book of Exodus, especially Chapters 1 to 20, 32 and 33, and partially in the Book of Numbers. Throughout his mission, Moses no doubt felt the full burden of leadership and suffered the penalties of leadership. At the end he experienced failure but was not downcast over it. He stood at the borders of the Promised Land, looked into the land of his forefathers, Canaan, a land flowing with milk and honey. And yet he and his people were prevented from entering it: "I have let you feast your eyes upon it, but you shall not cross over" (Deut 34:4). Moses was punished not for his infidelity but because he did not think God merciful enough to forgive his stubborn and backsliding people.

Moses, Man and Mediator

A poet has written that Moses is like a finger pointing to Christ. He was so important a figure in the Old Testament that he foreshadowed Christ. The formation of God's people Israel is impossible to understand without Moses. He was the teacher par excellence, the foremost of the prophets. And from Moses stem the traditions found in the Pentateuch. At the time of Christ, he was privileged to appear to the Apostles on the mount of Transfiguration.

Moses, like Christ, was a prophet, a redeemer, a mediator. Prophetically he acted as God's interpreter and explained to God's people the religious meaning behind the exodus event. Filled with the gift of messianic prophecy, Moses saw dimly ahead to the day when the Lord would raise up Christ as the Great Prophet (Deut 18:15). On Mt. Sinai he prophesied to his people, teaching them in God's name the Torah, the Law (though this term came to be applied to the first five books of the Bible or Pentateuch). It was really more than a set of laws that he gave them. It was a teaching containing words of life, a law of life and understanding which was to lead the people closer to God and convert them into a holy nation.

Moreover, Moses redeemed the Israelites from Egyptian slavery. His leading them through the Red Sea typified Christ's action in the sacrament of Baptism — freeing us from the slavery to sin and initiating us into His Church. As the Israelites were fed by the manna in the desert, so Christians are nourished spiritually by the Eucharistic Bread (cf. 1 Cor 10:1-4).

In the forty-year march in the desert, he repeatedly showed how God operates and communicates Himself through a mediator. He kept interceding with God for his people no matter how discontented this nomadic people was. The Hebrews generally recognized in a leader, were he king or prophet or priest, God's presence mediated to them, just as we might consider God's presence mediated to us in a saint living and working in our midst.

There is today a second exodus which was only preliminarily sketched out by the first. It is the new exodus of salvation-history. We are today the people of God making this spiritual exodus. We are under the leadership of Christ, who is a new, second Moses. As the Hebrews of old were delivered from Egypt under the leadership of Moses, so we are delivered by Christ from the slavery of sin and are led along the path of life to the promised land of heaven. As her faith prompted Israel to relive and reinterpret the historic event of the Exodus, so must the Christian relive and reinterpret the exodus of death to life in Christ.

The one trait in the character of Moses that I like so very much is his sense of the presence of God. Moses, in spite of his human failings, was a man close to God. It has been said that "no prophet ever had a greater sense of the presence of God." "Face to face I speak to him, plainly and not in riddles. The presence of the Lord he beholds" (Num 12:8). Pharaoh himself acknowledged the power of his prayer.

A lively sense of the presence of God was, however, a trait common to the Israelites. They were a theocratic nation, a nation ruled by God, and their mission in life was to be obedient to the divine will, to worship the true God and observe His law. They felt the divine nearness — in a cloud, in the desert, on the mountain, in thunder and lightning. God as it were pitched His tent among them; the tabernacle (= tent) was His place of dwelling.

Every good story has a moral. The moral of Moses' story is the fact of God's presence among His people. God is still present in every definable spot on earth. Otherwise a man like St. Francis of Assisi could not have found Him in the birds, flowers, fish, lambs, trees, fire. God's presence is hidden; He is the Invisible One; He never fails to be God-with-us.

IV

Joshua, the Valiant Leader

"My servant Moses is dead. So prepare to cross the Jordan here, with all the people, into the land I will give the Israelites. . . . I will be with you as I was with Moses: I will not leave you nor forsake you. Be firm and steadfast" (Jos 1:1-2, 5-6), so spoke the Lord to Joshua after Moses had died. Moses had led his people out of the land of Egypt to the edge of the Promised Land of Canaan. Before he died, both the Lord and he provided for a successor who was called Joshua, of the tribe of Ephraim, and it is his life and times that I should like to tell now.

Practically all of his story is told with much more detail and appeal in the book of Joshua, the sixth book of the Bible. The purpose of this book is to continue the salvation-history of the chosen people of God, after the death of Moses. The important chapters of the book, as far as our story goes, are 1 to 11 inclusive, and 23 and 24. The last chapters relate how concerned Joshua was to unify and consolidate the Israelites in obedience to and worship of Yahweh. It was the gist of his last message before death.

Before the Death of Moses

Let us have a look at the political and social situation in Canaan before we begin Joshua's life story. The land had been inhabited by Abraham and Jacob centuries earlier. At this date, about 1200 B.C., Canaan was under loose Egyptian rule. Raamses III was the Egyptian ruler in office. The Canaanites, who were nominally his subjects, were split into numerous tribes, none of which was on too friendly terms with its neighbors. They were morally corrupt, given to child sacrifice and sexual perversion even in the name of worship. Many of them were settled in independent city-states. About the only time they would endeavor to unite was to fight off a common enemy. Such was their condition as the Israelites stood looking eagerly toward the Canaanite border.

Joshua had been a personal friend and close companion to Moses during the exodus. While the two were tramping through the desert of the Sinai peninsula, Moses called upon Joshua's military skill and bravery to fight against Amalek (symbolic of evil) and put him to rout. This is the scene where Moses stands atop a hill overlooking the battle. As often as he prayerfully raises his arms (in the form of a cross), Joshua and his fighting men gain ground; as often as he lowers them they lose. Finally, Aaron and a companion think of the stratagem of supporting Moses' arms, and the Israelites win the battle.

Joshua proved himself in this battle. He was a valiant leader, well prepared to take command of an army, and gifted by Yahweh, who lays his plans for men carefully, with wisdom and ability and determination, qualities which go to make up leadership. The Bible (Ex 24:13 and elsewhere) calls him Moses' aide. He accompanied Moses to and from Mt. Sinai, went with him into the tabernacle of the covenant ("Meeting Tent," probably a leather tent-shrine, so called because it was there that they met with Yahweh and brought the people's requests), and was sent by Moses as one of the twelve spies to examine Canaan territory. Toward the end of his life Moses prayed for a successor. And Joshua was the leader proposed by Moses and commanded by the Lord to escort the people beyond the Jordan. You can read about his appointment in the Book of Numbers, Chapter 27. There Moses expresses the hope "that the Lord's community may not be like sheep without a shepherd" (Num 27:17).

The new shepherd was given the name "Joshua," a most appropriate name because in the original Hebrew it signifies "Savior" or "Yahweh is Salvation." Joshua was to save God's people by leading them into the Promised Land of Canaan, just as Jesus, whose name means "Savior" too, is to lead us into the Promised Land of heaven. The Fathers of the Church have seen a type of the Messiah in Joshua.

The Conquest of the Promised Land

South of the river Jordan Joshua marshaled about 40,000 fighting men, young and strong. For some forty years — a long time — God had made the Israelites wait to attempt a breakthrough into Canaan. They were forced to wait that long in punishment for their rebellious spirit — for refusing to believe the twin reports of Joshua and Caleb that Canaan was safe to enter. All the rebels in their midst had died in the meanwhile. In the new generation "there was not a man of those who had been registered by Moses and the priest Aaron in the census of the Israelites taken in the desert of Sinai" (Num 26:64). It was this new generation that stood within striking distance of Canaan. The young army had to fight manfully for every inch of its conquest. It was particularly skilled at open-field fighting, because it had all its training in the open desert land. But in Canaan there was need for attack upon fortified cities, which made its task harder.

The Israelites are said to have arrived in Canaan after 1229, during the transition period of the Bronze and Iron

Ages. The date is determined by the study of ancient pottery and the inscriptions on it.

The conquest had two phases. The first impression we get from reading about it is that it was sudden, bloody, and complete. There seem to have been three lightning-fast campaigns — through the center, then to the south and north, and all Canaan or Palestine was brought under control. But the opposite was actually the case. The conquest did go through the first phase, lasting about five years, when many tribes and city-states were captured. But because Joshua's army was too small, there were not sufficient forces to garrison a city after its capture. Later the same city had to be recaptured, sometime after the Promised Land had been divided by lots among the twelve Israelite tribes. Scholars estimate that the Israelites spent two centuries in conquest before they had a strong and permanent hold upon Canaan. Joshua therefore never saw his work finished.

The Crossing of the River Jordan

The first obstacle that faced Joshua and his men was the river Jordan. Ordinarily it swung twenty-five to fifty feet wide (later it was transformed by Christ into his own baptismal font). It was running high with flood waters, so high that it prevented the Israelites from crossing. It put them into the same predicament that they faced under Moses, only then it was the Red Sea that confronted them. The Bible expressly says that God worked a miracle that the Israelites might cross the Jordan. How the miracle happened we do not know. Clay banks might have toppled over, temporarily blocking the flow of water, and perhaps this was the phenomenon God used for the occasion. At any rate, as soon as the priests carrying the Ark of the Covenant stepped into the river, the current was immediately dammed up and the Israelites were able to cross a dry channel.

At this point of sacred history, and in fact throughout it, we should not overlook the significance of the Ark of the Covenant — that precious chest the people of God carried with them wherever they went. The Ark was carved out of precious wood and overlaid with gold, like an oversized tabernacle. The top of it was a mercy-seat, the throne where God established His invisible presence. The Ark contained the sacred things symbolizing the covenant Yahweh contracted with His people — the stone tablets of the Law, Aaron's staff, and a jar filled with manna. Our Christian belief in and devotion to the Eucharistic Presence nowadays compares well with the Hebrew affection for the Ark.

The Walls of Jericho Fall

It was essential for them that they be able to cross the Jordan in front of the city of Jericho, which guards the passes into the interior hill country. Jericho was a city well fortified with a double brick wall. Recent excavations have revealed that it was so well fortified that only a long siege would have taken it. Here we have the scene that has been set to music in the Negro spiritual, "Joshua fit de battle ob Jericho — an de walls came tumblin' down." It is true that Jericho's walls fell without a blow. The army tramped around the city once a day for six days; on the seventh day it was preceded by priests carrying the Ark of the Covenant, blowing trumpets, and a crowd shouting at the top of their lungs. But neither rhythmic marching nor sound waves collapsed the walls.

Yahweh's power was linked to the Ark, and it was in virtue of His powerful presence that Israel crossed the Jordan and captured Jericho. Yahweh and man, divine might and military strategy teaming up in this instance, were irresistible. God helps those who help themselves. The silent and strategic surrounding of the city was calculated to break down the morale of its citizens, and not its walls. Yahweh would take care of that, and He did, but not without using natural forces. The walls caved in and the army rushed in to kill man and beast. What force brought the walls down? An earthquake probably shattered part of the wall, leaving an opening for the army to enter. Earthquakes have been known to occur in Palestine. Before Joshua left the city behind he put a curse on its reconstruction.

From the victory at Jericho the army marched to a defeat at the settlement of Ai. The defeat was peculiar even though it was not long-lasting. The Israelites lost there because one of their number, Achan by name, disobeyed a divine ban by keeping for himself a part of the spoils taken at Jericho. This was not a case of one man suffering for the people, rather of the people suffering for one man, at least temporarily. The case evidences the keen sense of community spirit among the Israelites, of corporate solidarity as the biblical scholars call it — a sort of all-for-one and one-for-all spirit. The community had to suffer for the sin of one of its members, just as the community might benefit from the merit and example of a member. Nonetheless Achan had to die: "And all Israel stoned him (and his family) to death" (Jos 7:25).

Many, many other skirmishes took place during the course of the conquest, but the Bible tells none of them with enough detail to recount here. One other skirmish, the struggle over the Gibeonites, merits mention. The Gibeonites, a Canaanite tribe, sided and joined ranks with the Israelites, motivated perhaps by political expediency. When other tribes saw their defection to the enemy, they attacked. Joshua rounded up a rescue party for the Gibeonites and was able to gain a victory only because he prayed that the sun and moon stand still long enough to stave off the nightfall and allow the army to finish the fight. That standing still of the sun and moon has kept biblical scholars and scientists guessing as to what actually happened.

The Credit of Victory

Why were the Israelites able to win such a series of victories against the Canaanites? Militarily they were poorer (I say this not discounting the fact that military strategists have made special studies of Joshua's tactics). Culturally they were inferior. So what achieved victory for them? God had promised His people victory, and they in turn credited Him with the victories. They had the conviction that He would be faithful to His word, and they felt they were fighting for His cause. They kept before their minds the mission they had to fulfill — the conquest of Canaan. They had a religious zeal, the kind that later was to help the Christians win wars against the Moslems.

A second reason for their victorious conquest was that though the victory was a gift freely given by Yahweh, it had to be won by a long struggle. Every gift from God is worthy of our effort; every gift of His calls for response and cooperation on our part. Victory was for the Israelite nation a matter of militant cooperation between themselves and Yahweh.

At every stage of the long and weary trek from Egypt to the Promised Land of Canaan, the people of God set up altars and shrines of worship. After the exodus, during the desert march, and after the conquest, they stopped long enough to celebrate the paschal events in their worship. Their first camp and headquarters, where the Ark of the Covenant rested and the people worshiped, was Gilgal. From there the Ark was removed to Shiloh. Finally, toward the end of his life, Joshua summoned the people to worship at the Shechem sanctuary and altar.

Worship was one of the ways in which Joshua was able to confederate the people. Worship was the heart of the corporate life of the twelve tribes. They worshiped by feasting, by eating of the paschal meal, which reminded them of

God's gracious deeds, His Law and the oath of allegiance they owed to Him. Joshua must have been concerned about the people when he saw them enjoying a period of peace and their heroic fighting spirit beginning to wane. They began to toy with idolatry. By encouraging the worship of the one God, he hoped to revive their religious spirit.

The Twelvefold Division of Canaan

Once the Israelites were fairly well settled in Canaan, they could not rest upon their laurels. The land was divided by lot among the twelve tribes who stemmed from Jacob, for the twelve sons of Jacob had grown and organized into twelve clans or family units. It was but natural, I suppose, that they should experience the little differences, misunderstandings, jealousies, and quarrels that make up part of family and group life. Each tribe had problems and needs of its own. History betrays how weak and wavering they were.

They were unable to take possession of all the land at once, especially not of the fertile plains which were left to the Canaanites. They entered into mixed marriages with the Canaanites, a factor that weakened the opposition between them. They adopted from their pagan neighbors pagan modes of worship. They fell into sin and were punished by Yahweh. Their record is one of fluctuating between fidelity and infidelity to the God who was so faithful to His promises. Yet it was their common purpose to form one people and to stand united under Yahweh. We the people, they felt, must live under the government of God alone and according to His Law.

Joshua, Type of the Lord Jesus

The life and times of Joshua have a spiritual parallel to ours. Joshua is none other than Jesus our Lord. He has a command from God the Father to lead His Christian people to the Promised Land of heaven. The Promised Land will

yield an opening only if we take it by conquest: "The kingdom of heaven has been enduring violent assault, and the
violent have been seizing it by force" (Mt 11:12).

Symbolically we crossed the river Jordan the day its waters
were poured over our heads in the sacrament of Baptism
and we first stepped toward the Promised Land of heaven.
The Church writer Origen, paraphrasing 1 Corinthians 10:1–
2, draws a link between the Jordan and Baptism: "I would
not have you ignorant that all our fathers went through the
Jordan and were baptized into Jesus in the spirit and in the
river." Ever since we are to be a militant Church, fighting
the battle of Jericho until its fall, that is, until the world
collapses. Only by dint of hard effort, by the steady practice
of virtue and a continual life of grace can we pass over into
the Promised Land of heaven.

V

Ruth the Moabite

MRS. SOLANGE HERTZ, author of *Come Down, Zachaeus: Adventures in Scripture*, told a group of young women, "A spiritual woman goes about capturing God in precisely the same way she would capture a man. If you don't believe this, read the Book of Ruth." The fact is that Ruth did capture both God and her man. How she did so makes up the plot of one of the most lovely and enchanting stories of all ancient literature.

The Book of Ruth is not so much a book as a short story with an idyllic tone. Although divided into four chapters, the book should be read at one sitting in order to feel the full impact of its story. To read it serially (it is really too short for that) is to lose sight of its artistic plan and vivid detail. Because it was anonymously written, we can compare it with some of our folklore. The lesson it teaches is unmistakable: "How simple, kindly, God-fearing people ought to act in Israel," and, I might add, everywhere else.

You would catch me off my guard too were you to ask at once if it is a *true* story. Its story has threads of fiction interwoven with fact, as one finds in a historical novel or romance. It reports real fact based on an ancient tradition

kept within the Davidic family. Such a tradition is not at all
inconceivable seeing that Bedouins are clannish and hold
fast to such tales.

The Judges and Saviors of Israel

"Once in the time of the judges" — that is the delightful
way the story begins. That sort of introduction suggests that
the Ruth story forms a sort of complement to the Book of
Judges. The period of the judges begins about 1200 B.C. and
lasts about 180 years — up to the reign of Saul. The Ruth
story evolves probably in the second half of that period, when
the generation following Joshua's splits up selfishly, lives by
a spirit of isolationism, and becomes unfaithful to Yahweh
(Jgs 2:10–11; 3:7). Ruth stands in strong contrast to stories
of defection and immorality.

The judges were the saviors of the chosen people of Israel.
"Whenever the Lord raised up judges for them, he would
be with the judge and save them from the power of their
enemies as long as the judge lived" (Jgs 2:18). Men like
Gideon, Samson, Eli, Samuel, themselves filled with the
spirit of Yahweh, roused new courage in the chosen people,
emphatically pointed out their unique call in salvation-history,
and brought about religious reform. They took up the defense
of Israel without pay, position, or prestige. They were so
powerful militarily that no enemy would attempt a rematch
with them. They won tribal respect by their wisdom and
ability to judge and settle matters of dispute.

Under the Wings of Divine Providence

Repeatedly in its history, Israel was forced to emigrate by
severe famine caused by drought. The inhabitants were accustomed then to seek refuge in Egypt, Syria, or Moab.
When the famine hit the Bethlehemite Elimelech, his wife,
Naomi, and two sons, Mahlon and Chilion, the father moved
his family to the high plateau of Moab, east of the Dead Sea,

thirty miles or so distant from the hometown, Bethlehem. Moab was a land of non-Israelite faith and worship. That in itself must have led them to think twice before coming. But growling stomachs know no other law than survival.

The famine is only the first in a series of misfortunes befalling this Ephrathite family. After their arrival, Elimelech dies, leaving Naomi with her two sons. A bit of real history shows through our story when the two sons marry Moabite girls, one of whom was Ruth. Hebrew law forbade the marriage with a Moabite (cf. Deut 23:4). Thus history records the intermarriage of an Israelite with a Moabite, mixing Hebrew with gentile blood. What significance this intermarriage has we shall see later.

Within ten years the two sons die also. Now three are widowed. Not only is Naomi left husbandless and childless but she is also beyond the age that she can attract a second husband and bear other children. The heavy wings of Divine Providence enfold her life. But the shadow does not fall upon her without leaving a glimmer of hope. Rumors reach her that the famine has passed from her native land.

The Return to Bethlehem

Naomi's first intention is to leave without her daughters-in-law. On their part, Ruth and Orpah have almost every reason to stay behind. Naomi has no other sons whom, by right, they can claim to marry. They face the prospect of living in a foreign land among foreign people with a foreign faith. No, better to remain, for, as Naomi cautions them, "My lot is too bitter for you" (Ruth 1:13).

Although Naomi reasons this way with them, they feel an attachment and loyalty to their mother-in-law that must seem absurd to modern writers who play upon the theme of mother-in-law trouble. After some special pleading with them, Naomi convinces Orpah but not Ruth. The latter replies, "Do not ask me to abandon or forsake you! for wherever you go I will go, wherever you lodge I will lodge, your people shall be my people, and your God my God" (Ruth 1:16). There, in one sentence, you have the complete story of her conversion to the Hebrew people and the worship of the one true God. Needless to say, Naomi's influence on this girl was most wholesome.

The locale of their life together switches to Bethlehem. There they are met by the women of the city who, remembering Naomi's pleasant smile, are happy to welcome her back.

The Encounter With Boaz

The two widows arrived footsore and weary in time for the barley harvest. Ruth, friend and companion, felt it her duty to provide food for the elderly Naomi and asked permission to glean the leftovers from the harvesters. The humane custom was to permit the poor to glean the remains of the harvest. Naomi consented. It was then that Divine Providence took another hand in Ruth's life. She "happened" to enter the field owned by the wealthy farmer Boaz, to whom poverty had forced Naomi to sell her land. That Boaz proved to be one of Naomi's relatives, though not her next of kin.

Boaz's character revealed itself in his attitude toward his hired help and the widow Ruth. His deeply religious spirit expressed itself in his greeting to the workers, "The Lord be with you!" (Ruth 2:4.) We Christians who hear this greeting eight times during our Eucharistic worship are indebted to him for it.

To Ruth he was as gracious and considerate as any employer could be, making her feel at home, and even giving orders to his men to drop extra handfuls of grain for her to pick up more easily. He admired her for the generous-hearted care she gave to her mother-in-law: "May the Lord reward what you have done! May you receive a full reward from the Lord, the God of Israel, under whose wings you have come for refuge" (Ruth 2:12). In saying so to her, Boaz presented the theme of her story: virtue will not go without a divinely given reward.

Feminine Designs Upon Boaz

Late the same evening, after Naomi learned where Ruth had gleaned the barley, she informed her daughter-in-law of the relationship that existed between herself and Boaz and encouraged her to continue working in his fields until the end of the harvests. No evil would come to her there. And in the meanwhile, no doubt, Naomi began to formulate a plan. Why not have Ruth propose to Boaz Hebrew-fashion?

One night Ruth, by Naomi's orders, prettied herself up and stealthily laid down at the sleeping Boaz' feet. He woke with a start to find her there. Then she proposed to him, "Spread the corner of your cloak over me, for you are my next of kin" (Ruth 3:9). Boaz could not accept the proposal at once, because there was a still nearer kinsman who could lay claim to her. So he had to deal with the closer relative first.

The legality of the whole affair is not easy to unravel. Two Hebrew institutions combine to complicate the affair. First, there is the law permitting the nearest relative to buy or redeem the land and keep it within the family (cf. Lev 25:25). Then, since no sons of Naomi are left to Ruth for marriage, the nearest relative need not, strictly speaking, accept her (cf. Deut 25:5–10). But according to the law of goelship (a goel is a buyer or redeemer), the goel must take the woman along with the land. Both are in the bargain. And that is how Boaz explains the matter to the nearest kin: "Once you acquire the field from Naomi, you must take also Ruth the Maobite, the widow of the late heir, and raise up a family for the departed estate" (Ruth 4:5). The near relative wants the land but not Ruth, so Boaz can claim her for himself. The kin shows his refusal by taking off his sandal, as one nowadays might lose property by giving up a deed.

At one and the same time, Boaz is goel for Naomi by buying the land and goel for Elimelech by espousing Ruth and intending to perpetuate the name of the deceased.

Hebrew Family Life

Our story, ending rather abruptly in the Bible, allows us to imagine that "they lived happily ever after." But let us not rush into a conclusion. By stringing together further details of ancient Hebrew marriage, perhaps we can catch a glimpse of the Boaz-Ruth happy life.

In Hebrew family life the father played a big role, for family life was patriarchal. He was the center of the family circle, head or master of the family. To found a family, the husband had to build a home, for he united his family not merely by blood ties but by a family home. His family circle gradually widened to include the whole relationship, a clan, concentrated in one area though not necessarily in one village. He was like a modern father who might have relatives scattered throughout a county.

Members of his family called each other "brother" and had the duty to help and protect each other. Goelship was an institution which defined that duty. The goel was the defender and protector of the rights of property, liberty, and life. Thus it was as a vindicator of property that Boaz contracted marriage with Ruth.

In Israelite marriage the wife was subject to her husband almost like a slave to her master. The husband, however, did not treat his wife as a slave, for example, by selling her.

The wife did the hard work in the home — cooking and spinning — and in the fields. But this drudgery gained her respect and admiration both publicly and privately from her husband and children. She rose in prestige if she gave birth to children, especially if her firstborn was a boy. When we fully assess the role of wife in the Israelite family, we arrive at the conclusion that she was her husband's equal. No finer tribute was ever paid to a wife than what we read in Proverbs 31:10–31. Do you want to see a portrait of the ideal wife? Then by all means read that chapter in Proverbs.

The Birth of Obed

Ruth rejoiced the hearts of the deceased Elimelech's family when she gave birth to a son, Obed. This offspring came from the Lord, a blessing and signal honor (cf. Ruth 4:11–12). The Hebrew people recognized the tremendous dignity of woman — her power alone of giving life to a man.

In an act of adoption, Naomi clasped Ruth's child to her breast and claimed him as her own. She became his legal mother and Elimelech his legal father, though he was only their grandson. Through him the family name of Elimelech was kept alive. And so through the levirate (substitute or proxy) marriage of Boaz and Ruth, Elimelech's name was secured for posterity (cf. 2 Sam 14:7; 1 Sam 20:15).

Through the divine plan for mankind, Ruth, a non-Hebrew, came to belong to the family line of David (she was his great-grandmother), Mary, and Jesus. Matthew was careful to note this part of the genealogy of Jesus: "Boaz begot Obed of Ruth, Obed begot Jesse, Jesse begot David the king" (Ruth 4:17, 21; Mt 1:5). God's ways are not always our ways, so that out of seemingly small and everyday events he develops and fulfills an exalted future.

Just as Israel and Moab met in the marriage of Boaz and Ruth, so in Jesus did Hebrew and Gentile combine to make Him the Brother of us all under the common Fatherhood of God.

VI

King Saul

THE biblical story I am about to tell — I must forewarn you about it — is a tragedy. In the center of our imaginary stage stands a tragic figure. He can be compared with Macbeth, Hamlet, King Lear, Othello, for a characteristic of everyone of them is to be found in him. But he is more tragic than they, because he is so authentic. When we read his story beginning with Chapter 9 of the first Book of Samuel and ending with Chapter 1 of the second Book, or when we merely recall his tragic figure, we are struck with pity. We experience a mixed pathos of admiration and pity for the man who is King Saul.

The historical background of our story is set at the end of the period of the judges of Israel. We may say that Saul was the last of the judges and the first of the kings to rule over the people of God, the Israelites. Toward the close of this period the Israelites were ruled by the prophet and judge Samuel. He had grown old, and his sons, who were his likely successors, were unsatisfactory to the people. They kept clamoring for a king. "In those days there was no king in Israel; everyone did what he thought best" (Jgs 17:6). Samuel was vigorously opposed to the proposal at first, because he thought a kingdom meant the rejection of a theocratic nation, of a nation governed by Yahweh alone.

Easterners generally had high regard for a king and looked upon him as someone extraordinary, a sacred being who assumed divine power. Among the Israelites, once they had a king, royal prestige was beyond compare. His person was inviolable — no one dared raise a hand against him or curse him. He offered sacrifices and blessed the people. He was "the lamp of Israel" and their "breath of life."

Israelite Kingship

The Israelites may have adopted the idea of a king from their pagan neighbors. Should they have a king simply because the neighboring tribes had one? What advantage was there in a royal monarchy, a one-man rule, if that king were to interfere in Yahweh's kingship?

The period of the judges had been marked by successes and reversals, triumphs and defeats. Joshua had been able to knit the people only into a loose confederation. The spirit of national unity that had existed under Moses and Joshua was waning. At one point of their sacred history, the Israelites had even lost the Ark of the Covenant to the Philistines.

The Israelites did not fear losing religious unity under an earthly king. Yahweh would still remain their king. They felt the need of an earthly representative, a man selected from among themselves who would not misuse authority and lord it over them. He would not be a tyrant. Rather, he would weld the twelve tribes together tightly enough for them to fend off enemy attack. Militarily the adoption of a kingship was a wise move. Samuel, upon Yahweh's advice, conceded to it, but he expected the future king not only to achieve military success but to raise the standards of Israelite morality and belief. "And all the people cried and said: God save the king" (1 Sam 10:24).

Hence the kingship was to be no mere human setup, guided

by human wisdom and governed by human power. But its adoption was the beginning of the end of Israel. It was a sign among nations that Palestine belonged nationally to the Israelites — a nation among other nations. The emerging nation felt self-confident and self-reliant. After it fell, Israel became a wandering race again.

What sort of leader did Yahweh advise Samuel to pick? Saul was a member of the tribe of Benjamin — a tall, handsome son of a wealthy Benjaminite herdsman named Kish. "A fine figure of a man, none finer in Israel," translates Monsignor Knox; "he was a head and shoulders taller than any of his fellow-countrymen" (1 Sam 9:2). He was dignified and reserved, every inch a king. In age, he was between thirty-five and forty when he began to reign, and he reigned about fifteen years, from 1027 to 1012. Samuel anointed him king privately. He was to prove his worth before being proclaimed king publicly. By the anointing Saul became a consecrated leader, for anointing was a sacred rite. It meant that the king was dedicated to Yahweh, that Yahweh in turn infused His Spirit into him so that he might fulfill his duty faithfully, and that Yahweh blessed his life and work. The anointing was, in a word, Yahweh's seal of approval upon His servant. Thus the sacramental anointing we receive nowadays reaches far back for its historical and religious value and meaning.

Saul quickly rose to the occasion to prove his mettle in a preliminary bout. He decided at once to fight the Ammonites. He rallied the people around himself and won the battle. The Ammonites were harassing the Israelites of Jabesh-gilead, a city of Transjordania. The citizens of that city, as we shall see later, never forgot Saul's good turn.

War With the Philistines

Saul had bigger military ambitions. Once he had tasted a bit of victory, he ventured to take up the fight with the

Philistines, Israel's perennial enemies. "And there was a great war against the Philistines all the days of Saul" (1 Sam 14:52). Philistine raiding parties were continually plundering Israel. Their herds grazed in Israelite pastures. They wrecked the Shiloh sanctuary where the Ark of the Covenant was stored. They kept the Israelites militarily poor, allowing them only enough iron to forge out hoes, spades, and other farming implements, while they themselves had a monopoly in iron and controlled the technique of working with it. The iron industry was practically all theirs. Under Saul's regime the Israelites began to make use of it and to arm themselves with swords and spears. Saul was prepared to meet the Philistines with their own tactics in a sort of guerrilla warfare. He had 3000 men in his army and sent them upon raiding parties.

Saul's First Mistake

By this military strategy, and aided by a scary earth tremor, he was to score a temporary victory, but not before he committed his first tragic mistake. He did not want to enter battle before offering sacrifice to Yahweh and was awaiting the arrival of the priest-prophet Samuel. When Samuel did not appear for a week, on the seventh day, seeing that the people were dispersing, Saul went ahead and offered sacrifice himself. It was a terrible miscue: he had usurped priestly power. Perhaps Samuel felt that Saul was releasing himself from his prophetic control. Momentarily Saul had forgotten that his royal power should remain subordinate to and distinct from the theocratic power represented by the prophet. He pleaded the force of circumstances for an excuse, but that did not keep him from his tragic downfall. An evil spirit set into him. "But thy kingdom shall not continue. The Lord hath sought him a man according to his own heart" (1 Sam 13:14).

Temporarily, however, the Philistines were beaten and

withdrew. This gave Saul pause to collect a larger army. And in the meanwhile, the young shepherd of Bethlehem, David, was called to the king's side to soothe the royal feelings with his songs on the lyre or zither. The king's dark moods of depression and despair seized him more frequently.

The Israelites at home, especially the women, with singing and dancing, began to extol David over Saul because he had killed the giant Philistine, Goliath. "Saul hath slain his thousands, and David his ten thousands" (1 Sam 21:11). Saul's jealousy was stirred up, and it drove him to make attempts upon David's life. Once he would have pinned David against a wall with his lance had not David been quick enough to evade him. He dared David to kill a hundred Philistines single-handedly, hoping that he would be killed in the attempt. And for a reward he promised David the hand of his daughter, Michal. He asked Jonathan, his son, who loved and befriended David, to kill him.

At last Saul was so hostile that David was forced out of the royal court and into hiding. He and his family, together with social and political outcasts, formed a band of adventurers who hid in caves, in the clefts of hills. There he lived as a bandit chief at the head of an outlaw group. Like Robin Hood in Sherwood Forest, he gathered his band, swooped down from the hills, and pounced upon the Philistines unexpectedly, carrying on the fight in his own way. On at least two occasions he met up with and trapped Saul and could have killed him if he had not been led by respect and nobility of character to spare his life.

Poor Saul suffered from a persecution complex. His life was torn with jealousy, and his moods changed ever oftener. Instead of bending his efforts to score a complete and lasting victory over the Philistines, he wasted them seeking out David.

His Second Mistake

He was able to stage a successful combat against the Amalekites, but this was his last triumph, which eventually proved to be his undoing. He had actually carried on a holy war against the Amalekites and won a smashing victory. He had been commanded by Samuel to inflict a terrible sacred ban — not to spare a single man or beast (cf. Ex 17:14–16). What was commanded by Samuel — a war of extermination — was a barbaric act, or so it seems to modern minds, but it was no more barbaric than modern nuclear warfare.

Saul disobeyed. He permitted the Amalekite king to live and spared the life of select sheep and oxen. To massacre the Amalekites was to make a sort of offering of them to Yahweh, the Ruler and Judge of the living and the dead. Because Saul spared the defeated king and kept some choice animals, he was rejected altogether by Samuel and Yahweh. Saul, it seems, laid the blame to the people, who were going to use the spoils to offer sacrifice. Samuel remonstrated with Saul: "Does the Lord desire holocausts and victims, and not rather that the voice of the Lord should be obeyed? For obedience is better than sacrifices: and to hearken rather than to offer the fat of rams" (1 Sam 15:22).

While Saul was busy fighting the Amalekites and dissipating his military energy on David — chasing him and creating a schism in Israel, the Philistines were gaining strength. They gathered on the plain of Esdraelon, a field about sixteen miles long, stretching north and south, shaped somewhat like a triangle. Saul was not emotionally fit to take up arms against the Philistines. His guerrilla attacks were at least temporarily successful, but now, when he saw their tremendous military power, he despaired. He could no longer consult Samuel, for he was dead. Like Macbeth, Saul had recourse to a witch for superhuman guidance. Samuel's spirit appeared to him, reproached him for his disobedience, and predicted his downfall. Saul could have avoided defeat, but he was so

desperate that he entered a pitched battle and staked his
life on a final showdown. In the last fight his three sons were
killed, Jonathan too. As Saul saw the oncoming defeat and
humiliation, he asked his armor-bearer to take his life. The
latter refused to lay hands on the Lord's anointed. And Saul
fell on his own sword, a suicide.

The Character of Saul

Saul, although never dealing the Philistines a knockout
blow, was able nevertheless to establish the kingdom of
Israel once and for all. We must admire that tall, noble
figure, intelligent and energetic leader, brave general. A man
of decision and, until late in life, master of self. He was
religious at heart. He and his men sometimes fasted in
preparation for a battle and bettered their prayers for aid
from Yahweh. His falling out with Samuel, the prophet and
judge, must have worried him no little. Samuel's prediction
that God would abandon him must have preyed on his
mind. He had a fixed idea that everyone around him was
betraying him, and that fancy aggravated the burdens of his
office.

He was, sadly enough, emotionally unstable. The pendu-
lum of jealous and hateful feelings kept swinging from one
extreme to the other. And yet, as king, he lead a simple,
rustic life. He built no colossal palace. He had no harem, as
Solomon was to have later. His home was in a small country
town that had no future. He surrounded himself with officials
from his own small tribe.

Despite his weaknesses he was popular among his people.
The townspeople of Jabesh-gilead whom, early in his career,
he rescued from the Philistines, loved him to the end and
risked sending men to steal his body and give it decent burial.
He had the respect of his general, Abner. His armor-bearer
refused to kill him. And David himself never lost admiration

for him. The funeral hymn he wrote for Saul, which makes
up the first chapter of the second Book of Samuel, is the
finest in the Old Testament. "Saul and Jonathan, lovely, and
comely in their life, even in death they were not divided. . . .
How are the valiant fallen, and the weapons of war perished?"
(1:23, 27.)

Lessons in Virtue and Vice

What lessons, if any, can a tragic figure such as Saul teach
us — three thousand years later? I believe that the good and
bad points of his leadership present a memorable picture to
us. All of us Christians are called, in one way or another,
by the royal anointing we receive in baptism and confirma-
tion, to be leaders. Whatever our life and work, we have the
sacramental potential for leadership. We simply cannot wait
for some far-off future opportunity to show our infused qualities of leadership. The opportunity is here and now. Saul —
let it be said to his credit — started from where he was: the
tall, towering son of a Benjaminite in search for his father's
lost cattle.

Saul's mistakes are repeatable. He failed because of his
self-interest, because of the jealousy that was gnawing at his
heart. His fight with David wasted his energies; jealousy is
bound to sap anyone's strength. Perhaps he let the strong
wine of leadership go to his head when he was supposed to
be a servant of servants. In his disobedient spirit he sought
out no help or was impatient of it, and did not employ the
talents of Samuel and David to the full and have them share
his responsibility. Saul found it impossible to organize a
one-man army, just as today the militant Church is not a
one-man Body.

Leadership is most and always in demand in the unwanted
job. At his position Saul undoubtedly felt loneliness and dis-
couragement, and yet he had a spirit of stick-to-it-ness. He

bore the burden of trying to unite twelve tribes who had to forgo some of their independence for the sake of a common strength and common good.

The penalties of leadership are trouble, problems, disappointments, hardships, misunderstandings. But Saul was tricked into thinking and seeing traitors everywhere. One can win by losing. To accept a job and do it to the best of one's ability, yet seemingly fail at it, is actually to win. "He who would save his life will lose it; but he who loses his life for my sake will find it" (Mt 16:25). If Saul had not oversupervised and finally taken his life, he would have won by losing it.

VII

David the Beloved

PICK up the Gospel by Matthew and at the very head of it you will find the family tree of Jesus traced to King David. There Jesus is called the "Son of David." And the Book of the Apocalypse, more than once, links Jesus with David. Jesus is to have and hold the key of David, he is the root of David, and he is quoted, "I am the root and offspring of David" (22:16).

About a thousand years before Christ, David had been a type of the Messiah. By "type" I mean a rough sketch of what was to come.

David was an ideal king. He was to establish the kingdom of Israel, the house of David, and that kingdom was to be ruled for a while by a Davidic dynasty, that is, the rule was to continue within the family. God willed eventually to put an end to the earthly kingdom of Israel and of David's family. But another David would come to reestablish the kingdom for eternity. The other, David II, was Christ, who founded the new kingdom of His Church, filled with justice, loving-kindness, peace, and security. His kingdom will stretch over the whole world.

So Christ, in reaching back a thousand years to identify

Himself with David, had more than a physical link in mind. He was to set up a kingdom for which Israel was only a preparation. This is why the name of David appears so often in the New Testament history of the kingdom of the Church. His importance in sacred history cannot be overestimated.

The Years in Saul's Court

David was born in the very town in which the Messiah was to be born, the town of Bethlehem. He became a shepherd lad who tended his father's flocks near Bethlehem. The Bible describes his features for us. He was ruddy-faced, "beautiful to behold, and of a comely face" (1 Sam 16:12, 17:42). His fame as a skillful string artist reached King Saul's ears, and he was called to the king's side to soothe him in his melancholy moods. He must have been a most likable lad, with a winning and lovable personality. He won the friendship of the king and his son Jonathan.

According to ancient custom — and it was not a bad idea at that — all-out war between two countries was forestalled by engaging two volunteer and representative men in single combat. Possessing enormous strength and relying upon Yahweh's help, David challenged and single-handedly slew the nine-foot giant Philistine, Goliath (1 Sam 17:8–10). He was a valiant soldier: to win the hand of Michal, Saul's daughter, he killed a hundred Philistines. He had such clever ways in diplomacy and society that he was able to rule by love, without force or fear, so that no one was disloyal to him. The ideal king.

As a matter of fact, he was such a likely candidate for the kingship that Saul grew jealous of him and drove him out of the royal court. Jonathan convinced him to leave and stay in exile, warning him that reconciliation with Saul was impossible. Later Saul died by his own hand. David was thirty when he laid claim at Hebron to the kingdom of Judah, to which tribe he by right belonged. He was anointed by Samuel publicly and solemnly. Because he belonged to the tribe of Judah, he was a southerner. The rest of the tribal peoples were northerners, and they were governed by one of Saul's sons, Ishbosheth.

The Fight Against the Philistines

When David went into office, Israel was still facing Philistine attack. The situation in Israel bordered on the hopeless. At first the Philistines favored the idea of David's kingship, as they felt him to be their ally. As long as David confined his reign to the south and thus kept the rift open between the north and south, the Philistines had nothing to fear. The antagonism between the northerners and southerners was long-standing.

The Philistines held the principle, "Divide and conquer." But they became alarmed on seeing David gain control over all Israel. Ishbosheth was a weakling, and the Israelites in the north soon learned this. They began to side with David because he was capable of giving them inspired leadership and had successes to prove it. In two attempts to cut David off from the northern tribes, the Philistines failed. David was wise enough to adopt Saul's guerrilla tactics against them. Not only was David no longer their vassal-subject, but he began to take the offensive and pushed the fight into their own territory southwest of Jerusalem. After more than 200 years of incessant warfare, they were a subdued nation; they no longer menaced Israel's borders. And since David made no effort to rule over them, in time friendly relations developed with them.

David's reign at Hebron, lasting seven and a half years, was marred by wars. They were nonetheless turned into triumphs for David because the Lord fought openly on the side of Israel. His wars successfully made Israel an independent state.

David was the first to acknowledge that God was with

him; he was a king according to God's heart. His royalty was theocratic, that is to say, subordinate to the Lord's rule. To walk in the ways of David meant to obey God's will. As a king, David stood under the judgment of God and was responsible to him. This was a situation unique in the history of kingships, where the principle "the king can do no wrong" was intolerable. Kingship was under Yahweh, which meant that Yahweh had entered into a covenant with David. In due time the covenant would issue into a worldwide kingdom of love, peace, and justice under the Messianic King, the Son of God.

The Capital at Jerusalem

Without a doubt, David's great achievement was to unify and consolidate the Hebrew empire by setting up a monarchy and heading a dynasty. He concentrated power in his own hands. His master stroke was a compromise. He knew that Hebron, situated too far south, was a city unsatisfactory to the northerners. His choice of the citadel Jerusalem (Zion), a city he had taken from the Philistines, was a compromise. It lay almost in the center of Israel, centrally and neutrally located between the north and the south, and strategically set along the caravan route between Syria and Egypt, and between the East and the Mediterranean. Even afterward this capital of all Israel was to be known as the City of David.

We can hardly imagine how important the city was to the Israelites. It impressed them more than our modern metropolis does us — New York, London, even Rome, and more than the ancient cities of Athens and Constantinople. At one time its size was much smaller than the modern city — about two city blocks long, covering eight acres in all. But to the Israelites it was a symbol not only of national spirit and power but, as we shall see, of the presence of Yahweh. Its importance was, briefly, civic and religious.

Saul had lived a simple, rustic life. Not so David. At

Jerusalem he began to build up the capital, court, and palace — the externals of his kingdom. He built a splendid court according to the oriental mentality and surrounded himself with many officials. He appointed a commander in chief of the army, a secretary of state, diplomats, advisors, a royal bodyguard, like the Secret Service or the Swiss Guard, and others. He had an eye to posterity and a sense of history, for he designated scribes (secretaries) and recorders to keep minutes of the important affairs of state. They are the source from which we draw so much of Davidic history: "Now the rest of the acts of —, and all his wars, and his works, are written in the book of the kings of Israel and Judah" (2 Chron 27:7).

His bureaucracy was patterned after the Egyptian models. He took to himself a big harem, which not only helped him to raise a large family but, because he took wives from neighboring tribes, helped him to establish family ties with them.

Jerusalem, the Religious Center

Besides being the symbol of his nation, David wanted Jerusalem to be its religious center, and nothing could have pleased the people more. But how was he to accomplish this feat? Religious-minded as he was, he brought the Ark of the Covenant, which Saul had so much neglected, to the city in a solemn and military procession (2 Sam 6:12). The Ark was brought from Kiriath-jearim to Jerusalem, and thereafter Jerusalem was known to be not merely the City of David but the City of God, the Holy City, the City where God dwelt. David arranged for a complete musical court to give continual praise to the Lord.

Up to that time the Ark had been kept under a tent-shrine to shield it against the weather and misuse. David felt it improper that he should live in a royal palace, huge and splendid, while God should have only a tent for His dwelling place. That is why he planned to build a temple for the Ark.

He collected money and materials for it, bought property and erected an altar on the site. But Nathan the prophet disappointed David with the prediction that the task of building the temple would fall to his successor. The Lord told David, "Thou canst not build a house to my name, after shedding so much blood before me" (1 Chron 22:8). David's piety was rewarded anyhow: God promised that He would establish His kingdom forever. How little David knew what that kingdom was to be!

David's Sin and Repentance

He was at the height of his power and glory when he committed the first of the two big sins of his life (cf. 2 Sam 11). The first made him infamous and famous at one and the same time, infamous for the sin and famous for the repentance afterward. He fell into the sin of adultery with Bathsheba, the wife of Uriah, one of his officers. The sin took place while Uriah was on the battlefield. David sent word that Uriah should take a leave of absence because he knew that Bathsheba was pregnant, and he wanted Uriah to think the child was his. When Uriah refused, he ordered him to be sent to the front lines where he was left unguarded and was killed.

So did he heap one sin upon another. The Lord then sent the prophet Nathan to call David to account for his crime. Some time passed before David repented of his sin, but what a repentance that was! It showed definitely the greatness of the man. Yahweh pardoned him because He saw his sincere contrition, yet left him with penalties to suffer. Sin, whatever kind it is, seems to have a built-in punishment. David's sin was punished by the child's death seven days after birth. David wholeheartedly accepted the penalty and became a model of penitents. Somehow poetic justice was even done to poor Bathsheba; it was her other son by David, Solomon, who was to succeed his father to the throne of Israel.

Sensuality was not the only sin for which David had to pay dearly. He also sinned by pride in resolving to take a census of his people. The census seemed to him the political thing to do to maintain a standing army, draft soldiers, and impose taxes. To the Hebrew mind, however, census-taking signified that the kingdom belonged to the king and not to the Lord. In consequence the Lord punished David again. He had to be brought up in the school of suffering. He and his people suffered a famine for three years, a pestilence for three days, during which 70,000 died. Then the Lord stopped the pestilence.

Judgment Over His Reign

David reigned at Jerusalem for over thirty years, to make a total of about forty years in the kingship. His royal career, to say the least, was checkered. It rose up to the mountain of success and dipped into the valley of suffering, trial, war. It was the longest and strongest in the history of Israel. David was still in the prime of life when his wars of conquest were over, but his last years were troubled with family intrigue, violence, and rebellion.

Tamar, his daughter, was raped. His sons, especially Absalom who contended for the throne, brought sorrow and shame to him in his declining years. Absalom went so far as to begin at Hebron a campaign against his father. He collected an army of malcontents and for a time held Jerusalem captive, while his father fled from the city. Some of Saul's followers belonged to the revolutionaries and welcomed the chance to get even with David. Their revolt, plus the violence and murder within the family circle, saddened David's last days.

At seventy, David was a broken man, weak, bedridden. His strength was wasted with sensuality, wars, family quarrels,

civil strife. And yet he still had to see to the appointment
of a successor. When he found out that Adonijah, his oldest
son, had royal ambitions, he decided against him and under
pressure from Bathsheba, his favorite wife, and Nathan the
prophet, announced that Solomon was his choice as successor. The choice was not easy, for in choosing Solomon
he was not choosing his oldest son, and yet he was inaugu-
rating a dynasty. The Hebrew people were not quite ready
to accept one of David's sons for a successor. The idea of a
dynasty ruling over them was still too novel for them to
take to it without grumbling. It was virtually David's last
official act.

The Davidic Psalms

We should not quit his life story without taking note of
a piece of his work that has been handed down to us and
is a literary treasure to this day. The work is a masterpiece,
the product or fruit of his great poetic talent. David was a
poet-king. Bits of his poetry, or poetry attributed to him
because it has characteristics of his style and age, are sprinkled
throughout the liturgy. Hardly a Mass is without it.

I refer to the psalms, of course. In the original Hebrew
the word "psalm" means "song of praise and thanksgiving."
The psalms sing of God's goodness, His power and mercy.
"Taste and see how good the Lord is; happy the man who
takes refuge in him" (33:9). They are full of the thought
of God, of His presence in the world of His making, the
history of His people. They vividly portray David's grief and
lament. If understood well, they have an appeal to every
soul. They proclaim the glory of Jerusalem, the glory of Zion,
and sound overtones of praise for the new Jerusalem which
is the Church of today. Later in its history Jerusalem was
to be destroyed, and its destruction signified the end of the
Israelite era. The old order of things was giving way to the
new. The Church became the new Israel.

A Man of Piety

Undoubtedly David, in contrast to Saul, was a man of piety; he had deep and strong religious convictions. This trait is exemplified especially in his care for the Ark of the Covenant. When it was brought in procession to Jerusalem, he took part in that procession. Publicly, in the sight of his people, to a tambourine accompaniment, he danced "with all his might" in front of it — danced in the presence of God.

We can scarcely conceive the Hebrew devotion to that Ark. Perhaps it was as meaningful to the Hebrews as the presence of the Blessed Sacrament is to us. When the Ark was in their midst, Yahweh was present with them. United in prayer and sacrifice before the Ark, the twelve Hebrew tribes better comprehended how they were brothers in origin, tradition, and faith. David's order therefore to have the Ark transferred to Jerusalem was no mere political move, even if it was a unifying factor for the Israelite nation. The move reflected the religious feeling of the man: "How shall the ark of the Lord come to me?" (2 Sam 6:9.)

One other quality of his was more outstanding, I think. After sinning grievously, David confessed humbly to his sin. God saw into his sincerity and readily forgave the sin: "And David said to Nathan, 'I have sinned against the Lord.' And Nathan said to David, 'The Lord hath taken away thy sin'" (1 Sam 12:13). Psalm 50 (51), the *Miserere*, full of the sentiments of a truly repentant man, has become the Church's prayer of penance. And many another psalm contains a plea for mercy.

The sincerity of David's repentance can be seen from his readiness to accept punishment for sin and to forgive others the faults which he recognized in himself. He did not grumble against the will of God. In fact, he was willing to relieve his people from the burden of punishment and to take it upon himself. It was not the self-imposed penance that counted the most in his sight. He experienced, by way of anticipation, the daily cross that God places upon human shoulders, the cross which makes men worthy of the Messiah.

It is impossible within this short scope to narrate all the events of David's life. For the full story of this holy king I refer you to 1 Sam 16–31:13; 2 Sam; 1 Kings 1–2:12; 1 Chron 10–29:30, and the Psalms.

VIII

Elijah the Tishbite

OUR Lord had to condition His apostles for His terrifying passion and death on the cross. One of the means He chose was His Transfiguration on Mt. Tabor. Jesus led Peter, James, and John, three bosom friends, up the high mountain and let them see what was usually veiled to them, the glory of His Godhead. His face shone brilliantly, and the whole brilliance of the vision bleached His garments white as snow.

The two men seen in the vision speaking with Jesus were Moses and Elijah, the representatives of the Old Law and the Prophets. Peter was so dazzled and dumb struck that when he came to his senses he blurted out, "Rabbi, it is good for us to be here" (Mk 9:4). And he immediately wanted to set up three tents to commemorate the event.

Later in life he was to remember the event and rehearse it for his people. The voice of the Father spoke to them at the time, "This is my beloved Son; hear him" (Mk 9:6). As if to say: In days of old you Hebrews used to listen to Moses and Elijah. Now you must hear My Son, for He confirms everything taught by Moses and Elijah and all the prophets. He continues and harmonizes and fulfills the Old Law, and personifies the New. The same plea for a hearing from His compatriots was made by Jesus Himself, "Do not think that

I have come to destroy the Law or the Prophets. I have not come to destroy, but to fulfill" (Mt 5:17).

The Elusive Prophet

Elijah is the man in the vision who catches our fancy now in this sweep of salvation-history. We need to resort to a flashback to see him, but keep your eyes peeled for him, because he is so elusive and surprising. He is quick to appear and disappear, the sort of character who dashes in and out of the human scene, amid fire and rain, not without leaving a great and good impact. He seems to play the old-fashioned game of hide-and-seek. How he squeezed into the Transfiguration incident is, in a way — because Moses was a prophet too — a quirk of sacred history. His sudden comings and goings symbolize God's direct hand in human history.

For the greater part of his life story we need to consult the first and second Books of Kings (third and fourth Books according to the Vulgate numbering). If you are interested in tracking him down, picking up scanty clues along the way, then you will read about him in the first Book of Kings, Chapters 17 to 19, and Chapter 21; then in the second Book, Chapters 1 and 2.

Elijah is a rough and hardy character, reminding one of John the Baptist, who some thought was his reincarnation. Like John the Baptist, Elijah is a son of the desert. He is dressed in a skin garment drawn tight about his waist by a leather girdle. Over his shoulders is draped a hairy mantle — the distinguishing garb of a prophet. Mostly he makes his home in river grottoes or mountain caves, where he often has to hide. He almost always sleeps in scanty shelter.

His name in Hebrew reveals something of his greatness and the majesty of his prophetic role; it means "My God is Yahweh." Throughout his life and works he defends the Hebrew faith in the one true God. Scripture compares him to a fire and his spoken word to a burning torch: "Till like a fire there appeared the prophet whose words were as a flaming furnace" (Sir 48:1). The highest praise that could be paid Elijah was to be called "a man of God," which in our terms means that he was a saint.

Elijah appeared in Hebrew history in the ninth century before Christ, neither the first prophet nor the last. Moses, we saw, began the long line of prophets. The times in which Elijah appeared and disappeared demanded, more than ever, the gift of prophecy. The Hebrew people needed the prophet to prevent them from drifting away from their religion. Let us see why.

The Threat of Idolatry

David the king, by a stroke of religious genius, had united the twelve northern and southern tribes into one kingdom, setting up a religious capital at Jerusalem. Solomon, his successor, built the magnificent temple in the same city. In many other ways, however, the latter sowed the seeds of division of the kingdom into north and south, into the kingdom of Israel in the north and the kingdom of Judah in the south. He imposed heavy taxes (he had to in order to finance his building program), forced men into labor, married and fell under the influence of so many pagan wives that he opened the gates of Jerusalem to pagan religions. As a result, the people were constantly faced with the danger of compromising their religion.

The kingdom was actually divided in 922. The northerners built a pagan sanctuary (at first two shrines honoring golden bulls, then later a sanctuary) at Samaria. Pagan religions infiltrated like a fifth column into Hebrew life, becoming the great danger and threat of the day, and a danger that had to be met.

The danger worsened when Ahab was king in the north, with his capital at Samaria. Scripture states the truth bluntly, "And Ahab did more to provoke the Lord, the God of Israel,

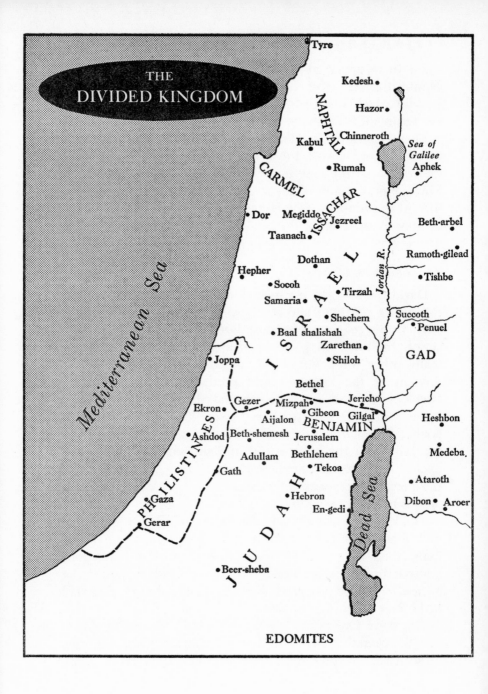

than all the kings of Israel that were before him" (1 Kings 16:33). His marriage to Jezebel was a religious failure but a political success, a very expedient wedding. Through marriage with that notorious woman he was able to cement friendly and political relations with Phoenicia, a great commercial center. But for her nuptial reprisals, the aggressive Jezebel killed worthy prophets and destroyed altars erected in Yahweh's honor. As commerce and trade with Phoenicia spelled ruin for the Israelite religion, the battle between the prophet and queen was on. Elijah stepped into the scene and announced that a three-year draught would fall upon Phoenicia and Israel.

It was not only commerce and trade that tempted the Israelites away from their religion; it was the Canaanite religion itself which Jezebel professed. Discoveries of Canaanite literary remains made in 1930 have given us a better picture of the Canaanite religion. Baal was the greatest of its gods, the lord of sky and weather. His voice was thunder. All earth and human fertility were due to him. When he supposedly died, famine and sterility fell upon the earth. When a goddess conquered death, he returned to life, and then once again the earth became fertile.

The reason the Israelites could so easily be influenced by these myths was that agriculture was their livelihood. The evidence is at hand that they lapsed into the worship of Canaanite gods and goddesses; idols of goddesses of fertility were found among Hebrew possessions. Instead of keeping to the worship of the one God, they were lured into a sensual religion. Either out of deference to the queen or by force of agricultural necessity, many Israelites became Baal-worshipers.

The Prophetic Role

Elijah was sent by God at a time when the mass of the people had apostacized from Yahweh or were wavering between true and false worship. What was the role of the prophet in such a situation? The prophet did not necessarily predict the future, but he shaped it by revealing to his contemporaries the will and purpose of God. He read for them religious meaning and value into events of their day, his faith under divine enlightenment teaching him to see God's hand in human events. He was, in short, the mouthpiece of God and the transmitter of his message. He spoke in God's name and voiced His thought and plan. God wanted His plan of redemption to be realized in and through His people, people led by men who made known God's will. The prophet had a religious vocation — to serve God and His people. He had two functions therefore: to announce the divine plan and to see to its realization. He had to be faithful to God in his speech and by his example.

Generally speaking, the prophets were men of their time. By divine command they intervened in the course of history, took part in human politics. In good events they saw God's grace at work, in bad events they saw his punishment. They played upon the theme of life and death, the rise and fall of the Hebrew nation.

Throughout their history, the prophets were confronted with a double danger, narrowmindedness and formalism. They had to push the Hebrews to go beyond the letter of the law, to stop them from hardening their hearts and closing the mind to further progress. They always held up to the people the ideal of fulfillment and development. To combat formalism they preached the spirit over the letter, the end over the means, human conscience over routine and ritual. They were men of courage and conviction who did not tolerate compromise. Radicals in the true and good sense of the word, they rooted their religion in the one true God.

Life in Exile

The foregoing general description fits Elijah. His first step, as we already saw, was to check the inroads paganism was making into Hebrew life. Elijah felt successful when Israel was hit by the famine, but his triumph was short-lived. When Queen Jezebel grew angry and vowed to take his life, Elijah had to go into hiding.

It was during this first period of exile that Elijah was sent by God to the widow in the Phoenician town of Zarephath, from whom he was to get his meals. When he arrived at her home, he discovered that because of the famine she had hardly enough meal and oil to feed herself and her son. By divine power Elijah multiplied the meal and oil for the woman from that day forward, especially because she had been willing to share her poor table with him. The event shows a homey detail in the prophet's life, what a man of interest and love he was. While he was with her, her son died, and the widow began to feel that Elijah had brought calamity upon her home. He then breathed new life into the lad and raised him from the dead, symbolizing by his act the work of God, who is master of life and death. That was how he rewarded her hospitality and charity and made her recognize that he was a man of God.

In the meanwhile Ahab was trying to hunt up Elijah in order to have him put a stop to the drought. Finally God commanded Elijah to appear before Ahab and promised to send a rainfall. When the two met and spoke, they electrified the atmosphere with charge and countercharge. Ahab charged Elijah with troubling Israel with the drought (the king had hardly enough fodder to feed his chariot horses), and Elijah countercharged Ahab with the apostasy of the Israelite people. They decided to settle the matter between the storm-god Baal and Yahweh once and for all by a showdown between the two. Mt. Carmel, jutting into the Mediterranean Sea, was chosen for the site of the decisive contest. It was one man's faith in Yahweh pitted against the growing paganism represented by a group of four hundred and fifty false prophets, Jezebel's men, worshipers of Baal.

A large crowd of spectators was on hand. Two bulls were prepared for sacrifice. The God who would answer by fire and consume the victim would win out. The Baal worshipers cried out to their god, danced around the victim, and madly gashed themselves, but their orgy was to no avail. Elijah offered the sacrifice and prayed, and fire from heaven consumed the victim, the altar, and even the water lying in a trench around the altar. Earlier Elijah had reprimanded the people, "How long do you halt between two sides? If the Lord be God, follow him: but if Baal, then follow him" (1 Kings 18:21). What Elijah was really asking in more picturesque language was this: How long are you people going to do the splits — straddling the fence between Israel's faith and Baal's worship? Now the people began to shout, "The Lord he is God; the Lord is God" (1 Kings 18:39). In their enthusiasm they helped Elijah slaughter the four hundred and fifty false prophets. The drought and famine then came to an end.

On Mt. Sinai

Jezebel was furious when she heard about the slaughter of her prophet corporation. And again Elijah put on a disappearing act and fled for his life. This time he headed southward to Mt. Horeb, which earlier in salvation-history was called Mt. Sinai. It was the spot where God had made a covenant with Israel, which Israel abandoned — its altars ruined and its prophets killed.

Elijah was out of sorts; he wondered what he should do after the Carmel event. He prayed for the relief of death. God consoled and strengthened him with food and drink, and he walked "in the strength of that food forty days and forty nights" until he arrived at Mt. Horeb. (That food reminds us of the Bread of Life which is able to strengthen us on our journey through the desert of this life.) On Mt. Horeb God comforted Elijah by appearing to him amid wind, earthquake, and fire. As Moses did before him, Elijah stood at the mouth of a cave, shielding his eyes with his hairy mantle. Then God ordered him to anoint two kings and appoint a prophet to succeed himself.

Elijah's sense of duty and social justice were always getting him into trouble. Let me relate one more incident to the point. A certain Naboth had a vineyard adjoining the royal estate. Ahab fixed a jealous eye on it and would have bought it if Naboth had only been willing to sell. Jezebel used her cunning to trump up a case of blasphemy against Naboth, and on that false charge he was stoned to death. When Elijah, the champion of social right and order, heard of the crime, he predicted that dogs would lick Ahab's blood and eat Jezebel. Their children would die and be the prey of vultures.

The final scene presents him journeying with Elisha, the prophet who was to succeed him. He had symbolized giving him the gift of prophecy by placing his mantle over him. Elisha was a well-to-do farmer, busy plowing, when Elijah called him to his side, and Elisha kept him company until his swift departure. Without waiting for death, Elijah was swept from this earth in a fiery chariot drawn by fiery horses.

The Return of Elijah

Elijah is considered to be the loftiest and most wonderful prophet of the Old Testament, and he figures prominently in the New. Christ, when questioned about His identity, had to deny that He was Elijah. The common belief was that Elijah would reappear: "Elijah is to come first and will restore all things" (Mk 9:11). "But I say to you that Elijah has come" (Mk 9:12). Our Lord was saying that Elijah came in the person of John the Baptist. In a deeper sense He implied that He Himself was the true Elijah who raised to life the son of the widow of Naim, and the new Elijah who witnessed to God's ways, a prophet and worker of miracles.

Be that as it may, we have seen that Elijah was a real prophet, a servant of Yahweh and messenger of His. No easy compromiser, but a man with a call from God and a mission in life. He responded to that call without considering the cost to himself. He knew his duty, did not flinch from it despite the fact that it offered him no earthly reward or political advantage. He had the common good of the Hebrew people at heart, even though he felt the sting of public disapproval and the hatred and scheming of a queen. Surely he was a prophet unacceptable in his own country.

Prophecy and Vocation

Two features of his life are very much like ours. One is the call to a life with God, to be spent for His cause. Any such call to the Christian life is a dear gift which one can hardly value enough. But the call is constant, daily, to be heard in every nook and corner and never to be silenced or hid from. To be a Christian is to accept the prophetic role of interpreting events of the day by Christian principles and teaching Christianity by word and example — at prayer, work, recreation.

On the other hand, Elijah could not escape the weariness of his duty and the continual combat against paganism, nor can we. The tug of worldliness would lead us to a soft compromise, the very thing that Elijah fought against with heart and soul. To compromise with the sinful world is to grow stale, to let well enough alone, to allow the letter of the law to rule over the spirit. Such a course of action gradually leads to religious discontent. The Christian life, because it is partially prophetic, is not without the hard and the difficult, which are not acceptable to the world. St. James, at the end of his epistle, remarks fittingly, "Elijah was a man like ourselves, subject to the same infirmities" (5:17).

IX

Isaiah, Greatest of the Prophets

In 1947, 1951, and 1952, the biblical world was rocked by the news of big discoveries in Jordan. Ancient manuscripts were found by bedouins and later by research scholars in a Judean desert, near the Dead Sea. Since that time the manuscripts have been called the Dead Sea Scrolls. They were discovered in ten caves, left there between the years A.D. 66–70. Among them were manuscripts of the Book of Isaiah a thousand years older than any we had of it before the discovery.

The Isaian scroll, written in Hebrew, is about one foot wide and about twenty-four feet in length. In addition, many other fragments of the prophet's writings were found. The scrolls give documentary proof that what we have of the Bible today, though it has been handed down to us through the Middle Ages, is kept whole and entire and suffers no serious gaps or losses. Researchers were able to date the writings from the pottery and coins found alongside them. The carbon 14 process was used to detect radioactive carbon which is present in all organic matter and helps to date manuscripts. Infrared photography helped to bring out illegible letters. And paleography, the study of forms and styles of writing, was used to trace authorship.

To whom did the manuscripts belong originally? To a Qumran community, a community of Essenes, members of a Jewish sect who lived together at the time of Christ. They had a community center or monastery where they gathered for study, writing, eating. They had a sort of postulancy and novitiate. Life was disciplinary, ascetic, and dedicated to the study and practice of the Old Testament law or Torah. The community had a special love for Isaiah and wanted to put into practice his saying, "In the desert prepare the way of the Lord!" (Is 40:3.)

The Triple Isaiah

Before we begin with Isaiah's life, let us have a look at the book ascribed to him, certainly the greatest prophetical book in the Old Testament. It is a kind of anthology, much of it poetical, made up of three parts. Only the first part was written by Isaiah himself, and it is called the First Isaiah, covering Chapters 1 to 39. The Second Isaiah was written almost three centuries later, while the Jews were exiled or displaced to Babylon, and it is contained in Chapters 40 to 55. This middle part is frequently called "The Book of Consolation." The Third Isaiah dates about a half century afterward, when the Jews had returned from exile. It extends to the rest of the book, Chapters 56 to 66. This division has to be kept in mind in order to understand the book as a whole, and even then the biblical scholars find passages hard to interpret.

The Call to Prophecy

The real and first Isaiah was born about the year 760 B.C. His name, as Hebrew names go, was very meaningful; it meant "Yahweh [the Lord] is salvation." Little is known about him or his family background, but hints are given that he belonged to a noble, high-ranking family in Jerusalem. He was a citizen of that city, and his writings reveal that he was a man of culture.

When he was about twenty years of age, the call came to him from God to enter a public, prophetic career, a career that lasted almost half a century, during the reign of four kings. In contrast to Moses and Jeremiah, Isaiah's answer to God's call was prompt. In the eighth century before Christ, reading and writing were fairly common, so that Isaiah, unlike the prophet Elijah, put his prophecy in writing so that God's word could reach a larger public. In this way his words could be read and meditated upon not only by his listeners but by others who had not heard him. Moreover, whatever he predicted of the future could be proved "black on white," as it were.

One day in his early twenties, Isaiah was in the temple at Jerusalem when God revealed Himself to him. God appeared to him in a vision, a giant robed figure on a throne, surrounded by angels. Isaiah was struck by God's holiness as he heard the angels chanting, "Holy, holy, holy is the Lord of hosts! All the earth is filled with his glory!" (Is 6:3.) The triple cry of "holy" was the Hebrew way of expressing God's holiness. To translate it into our mode of speech is to say that God is "most holy." The angelic chant is chorused daily by priests at the altar and by God's people in a dialogue or sung Mass.

The Holy One of Israel

In the Old Testament the God of our life is often presented to us as the God of justice (Amos) or the God of merciful love (Hosea). Isaiah was original in introducing us to the God of holiness, the King of tremendous majesty. The closer we draw to God, the truer will we find the Isaian conception of God to be.

God is neither all severity nor all tenderness. Because of His transcendent holiness, He refuses to be too familiar with us or to let us be free and easy with Him. When we encounter Him at prayer, we feel awe in His presence. He remains a mystery to us, the wholly Other, a mystery at once tremendous and fascinating. He can be so close to us at times and then again seem so far away, so present and yet so absent.

He makes us feel that He is Someone who is completely different from us. We cannot grasp Him. We cannot physically touch, approach, or see Him. God is a resplendent majesty and mysterious beauty, attracting us to Himself and keeping us in awe and at a distance. He is awe-inspiring and alluring at one and the same time. And that is why in a time of prayer we can be drawn to Him and yet feel a reluctance to pray. He leaves us speechless in His presence — we want to pray but cannot find the thoughts or words to describe our wonder and admiration, our praise and love.

God's holiness, then, judging from what Isaiah tells of his experience, is not only a matter of law or morality. To be holy as He is holy is to do more than obey His law. Holiness demands that men have faith in Him and in His plan of salvation. He alone has royal grandeur and power, He alone is sovereign. His holiness calls for a complete abandonment of the world to Him. Although Isaiah was a man of faith and vision, he was a realistic man of action too — faith commanding him to obedient action.

Man of Unclean Lips

The vision of God's holiness revealed to Isaiah his own sinfulness and made him cry out, "Woe is me, I am doomed! For I am a man of unclean lips, living among people of unclean lips; yet my eyes have seen the King, the Lord of hosts!" (Is 6:5.) Then Isaiah pictured one of the angels taking up a burning coal and with it purifying him and cauterizing his lips, rendering him worthy of his prophetic role. The prayer the priest recites at Mass before announcing the Gospel is modeled upon the angel's words: "See, now that this has touched your lips, your wickedness is removed, your sin purged" (Is 6:7). After such a purging, Isaiah was

ready to do the Lord's will: "Here I am, send me!" (Is 6:8.)
And to add resolution to his words, Isaiah wore penitential
clothing and walked barefoot for three years.

No Foreign Entanglements

But Isaiah's mission was doomed to fail. Let us see why.
In his day the people of God were a divided nation. A
northern kingdom, Israel, had split off from the southern
kingdom, Judah, to which Isaiah belonged. Before they divided they fought with each other in a not too brotherly
way. Then the northern kingdom of Israel fell into hostile
hands and was destroyed, an event that upset Judah itself.
Isaiah courageously predicted that if Judah played politics
with Assyria, a northeast nation setting out for world conquest, Judah itself would fall. Assyria aimed to control Asia
Minor and Egypt, and it wanted to use Judah as a stepping-
stone, a satellite nation. Isaiah issued one warning after
another against foreign entanglements, but the people turned
a deaf ear to him. The policy of neutrality that he preached
seemed impractical or inexpedient. Judah in such a case
would have to suffer martyrdom at the hands of the Assyrians.

Why did Isaiah remonstrate against foreign alliances? Because it meant that Judah would rely upon foreigners and
doubt Yahweh. Isaiah insisted that God is the Lord of history, and that all the people had to do was to rely upon
Him. He exhorted them to have trust in Yahweh: "Unless
your faith is firm you shall not be firm!" (Is 7:9.) Any contact with foreign (Gentile) peoples would lead to religious
contamination. But the people were blind, deaf, hardhearted.

The all-holy God did not blind, deafen, or harden their
hearts; they did it themselves. Isaiah wondered how long
God would have patience with them: "How long, O Lord?"
(Is 6:11.) Just as he contrasted his sinful self with his holy
God, so did he contrast the sinful people with God's holiness.
They needed to be cleansed from their sins to fulfill their

mission. "Come now, let us set things right, says the Lord: Though your sins be like scarlet, they may become white as snow; though they be crimson red, they may become white as wool. If you are willing, and obey, you shall eat the good things of the land; but if you refuse and resist, the sword shall consume you: for the mouth of the Lord has spoken!" (Is 1:18–20.)

A Spiritual Remnant

In spite of the gloomy outlook for his generation, Isaiah still had a spark of confidence burning in his heart to light a prospect of hope for God's people. God rules the world, and nations are but instruments in His hands. A remnant of the chosen people of God would remain faithful and inherit the future kingdom of justice and holiness, peace and prosperity. "The remnant of Israel, the survivors of the house of Jacob, will no more lean upon him who struck them; but they will lean upon the Lord, the Holy One of Israel, in truth. A remnant will return, the remnant of Jacob, to the mighty God. For though your people, O Israel, were like the sand of the sea, only a remnant of them will return; their destruction is decreed as overwhelming justice demands" (Is 10:20–22).

God intended to keep His promise to Abraham, Moses, and Isaiah — ever faithful to the bargain of love He had made with them. By preserving the remnant God kept alive in Israelite hearts their faith and trust in a coming Messiah. The small remnant would link together the Old with the New Testament and welcome the Messiah into the world. The small remnant would compose the early Church, that spiritual-minded community which would receive the Messiah. The Isaian vision thus merged the messianic hope with the peaceful and just kingdom of the Church.

Isaiah was so foresighted in his predictions that he has been called the "fifth" evangelist. His description of the future

Messiah is distinct enough to prepare the way for the revelation of His divinity. "A shoot shall sprout from the stump of Jesse, and from his roots a bud shall blossom. The spirit of the Lord shall rest upon him: a spirit of wisdom and of understanding, a spirit of counsel and of strength, a spirit of knowledge and of fear of the Lord, and his delight shall be the fear of the Lord" (Is 11:1–2). Isaiah is the Advent liturgist who prepares us for Christmas, announcing the birth of the Messiah. The Messiah, he says, will be Emmanuel (God-with-us), born of a young woman, a wonderful counselor, mighty God, the prince of peace, whose kingdom will be characterized by judgment and justice, kindness and faithfulness.

The Suffering Servant

The Book of Isaiah is not complete without the description of the future suffering Servant. Chapters 42–53 contain the famous four Servant-of-the-Lord songs (42:1–7; 49:1–6; 50:4–9; 52:13–53:12), which typify and extol the suffering Servant who will die for the sins of His people. His mission is to rid His people of their nationalistic ambitions, to open up a vista of salvation for all peoples. The suffering Servant is gentle and patient, a Man of ideals who faces the challenge of apparent failure. He is sustained by God in His physical and spiritual suffering. He has an obscure origin, looks unsightly, is burdened with pain, is alone and misunderstood.

If you have time, I would suggest that you take up and read Chapter 53, which will give you a sample taste of the rich wine of Isaian prophecy. "There was in him no stately bearing to make us look at him, nor appearance that would attract us to him. He was spurned and avoided by men, a man of suffering, accustomed to infirmity, one of those from whom men hide their faces, spurned, and we held him in no esteem. Yet it was our infirmities that he bore, our sufferings that he endured, while we thought of him as stricken, as one smitten by God and afflicted. But he was pierced for our offenses, crushed for our sins; upon him was the chastisement that makes us whole, by his stripes we were healed. We had all gone astray like sheep, each following his own way; but the Lord laid upon him the guilt of us all" (Is 53:2–6).

Isaiah himself, like the suffering Servant about whom he prophesied, met the fate of martyrdom. Sacred history reports that he was sawed in half during the reign of King Manasseh.

Fellowship in Suffering

It is only because we live in the new covenant of love that we know that Jesus is the real suffering Servant. He became the Servant of God upon earth by emptying Himself of His divine glory, and His emptying out led at length to death by crucifixion. His life was a ransom for many; He shed His lifeblood for many.

But, as Isaiah foresaw so long ago, the suffering Servant invited others to a fellowship in suffering. As if Isaiah's gaze became unsteady, his vision of the suffering Servant blurred over from the one to the many. Suffering has a social effect if the sufferer unites himself with the Servant.

Our first parent Adam, according to St. Paul's notion, represented the whole human race. So the Second Adam, the suffering Servant, represented us and we in turn represent Him when we are willing to suffer for God's people.

Nothing of human suffering is lost when a spiritual offering is made of it. No doubt, much suffering that has to be borne with is due to sin. Someone may be receiving double for his sins, but if so, the surplus can be a saving remedy for others. For such a one suffering is a great gift, especially if it is joined to that of the suffering Servant. "Because of his affliction," writes Isaiah, "he shall see the light in fullness of days" (Is 53:11). His day of glorification and supreme happiness is not far off. The dark, cloudy vision that Isaiah presents to his reader has the silver lining of hope shining through it.

X

Judith, the Heroic Jewess

"The more holy a woman is, the more woman she is," wrote Leon Bloy. After reading our story. I think you will agree that his observation fits Judith.

Judith is a legendary figure whose story in the Old Testament is founded on historical fact. It seems to have a historical event for a starting point but its value lies in its religious impact. A ball of yarn may have a rubber or cork center, but what is important is the yarn, not the center. If the story of Judith were written today, it would most probably take the form of a religious historical short story. There is not too much point then in trying to unravel the historical threads which make up this religious yarn. And yet they have a purpose; they give the story plausibility.

The single historical fact scholars have been able to find out with any certainty about the story of Judith is that the people of God were persecuted by the Egyptian ruler, Ptolemy VII, in the years following 145 b.c.

The ringleader in the story is given the name Nebuchadnezzar. He is called an Assyrian, but we learn from history that he actually was a Babylonian who began his reign in 605 b.c., seven years after Nineveh was destroyed (yet we

are told he ruled at Nineveh!). His forces battle it out with
Arphaxad, a king of the Medes who is unknown in history.
His general is Holofernes, a Persian who commanded the
forces of Artaxerxes III Ochus (358–337), 200 years after
Nebuchadnezzar's death. In 350 B.C., Holofernes passed
through Palestine and stopped long enough on his southward
march to Egypt to protect his flank. On his return home
from his successful campaign the general is decorated by his
king (but wait and see his outcome in the Judith story!).

Did the story teller(s) want to confuse listeners and readers with this hodgepodge of persons, facts, and dates? Seemingly not, because the story had to have a realistic background. The stage is set in the first half of the Book of
Judith (Chapters 1–7), so that we are prepared to accept her
heroic exploit (Chapters 8–16). No one knows how much detail, fanciful and true, was added in the retelling of her story.

Nebuchadnezzar the Villain

Historical or not, Nebuchadnezzar plays the part of the
villain. He is notorious in factual history for having destroyed
the city and temple of Jerusalem in 587 B.C., so what character could be more hateful to the Jews than he? His victory
over Arphaxad, the king of the Medes, spurs him on to spill
more blood. His troops move westward like locusts sweeping
over the land. His plan is "to bring all the earth under his
empire" (Jdt 2:3). He hires Holofernes to command his
armies: "Go out against all the kingdoms of the west, and
against them especially that despised my commandment
[to surrender unconditionally]" (Jdt 2:5). The only country
to withstand him is poor little Israel.

Why? Did she stand a chance of survival? Did she have
some secret weapon to blow Holofernes and his men to bits?
No, the reason was religious, not military. "For Nebuchadnezzar the king had commanded him [Holofernes] to destroy
all the gods of the earth; that he only might be called God

by those nations which could be brought under him by the power of Holofernes" (Jdt 3:13; 5:27, 29). The small Israelite nation, worshiping the one true God, could not afford to allow a usurper to take Yahweh's place. The Israelites had to oppose Nebuchadnezzar who represented all anti-God forces in the world. The odds were insurmountably against them; they had to face the enemy leader, his vast army, and the whole bloc of world empires (Assyria, Babylonia, Media, Persia — now the names of the Big Four become meaningful) who together symbolized the forces of paganism united against God.

God Versus Anti-God

The children of Israel in the land of Judah did whatever possible strategically to ward off the enemy. They guarded the mountaintops, built city walls, stopped up mountain gaps, and laid up provisions for defense. If need be, they were ready to slip down from the hills and meet the enemy on the plain of Esdraelon. This was the great battlefield of Palestine, at the foot of the mountain of Megiddo, or in Hebrew Armaggedon, where the fortunes of kings and countries were lost and won. In our story as in the Apocalypse (16:16) it has become symbolic of a fight to the finish between God and the powers of evil.

Israel did not rely upon military strength and position alone. She appealed to Yahweh for help and abetted her military with fastings and prayers. Joakim the high priest recounted how Moses won against Amalek "not by fighting with the sword, but by holy prayers." "And they all begged of God with all their heart, that he would visit his people Israel" (Jdt 4:12, 16).

Achior's Speech

When Israel's resistance was reported to Holofernes, he called in his Moabite and Ammonite auxiliaries to advise him about this stubborn people. The Ammonite Captain Achior spoke up and revealed the Achilles' heel of the Israelite people: "There was no one that triumphed over this people, but when they departed from the worship of the Lord their God" (Jdt 5:17). His advice was to inquire if Israel had failed in the sight of her God. "But if there be no offense . . . we cannot resist them, because their God will defend them: and we shall be a reproach to the whole earth" (Jdt 5:25). He was issuing fair warning, and his speech was preparatory to the climax of the Judith story. This point should be remembered.

At hearing this ominous report, the enemy once again asserts its colossal pride: "Nebuchadnezzar is god of the earth, and besides him there is no other" (Jdt 5:29). Holofernes grows violently angry and dispatches Achior to Bethulia, the Israelite camp, where he relates his experience and awaits his doom. The general's next move is to throw a blockade around the Jewish territory to starve out the inhabitants.

The Israelite situation turns from bad to worse until they decide that if no help be forthcoming from their God within five days, they will surrender to the enemy.

Enter Judith

Judith now hears about their defeatist attitude and, as if in answer to their prayers, in a long speech calls for patience and begins to bolster up their waning spirit. She, a woman among women traditional for their weakness, exemplifies courage while placing full trust in Yahweh. Her womanly instinct, vital and faithful, comes to the rescue in a situation where manly means and logic fail.

To grasp the meaning of her role, we must remember that women counted for little in ancient times. They could not enter the forefront of battle, still less did they hold responsible positions in civilized cities. They stayed in the background, confined to the home — spouse and mother. Judith was an exception to this ancient rule of life.

She was left a widow — but a wealthy, beautiful, religious widow. A valiant woman. She was one who had the ability of womankind to inspire confidence, stir up enthusiasm, and promote great causes under God — a deeply religious spirit. Her prayer to God to fortify her in her undertaking makes up Chapter 9 and even now, in translation, breathes the piety of Judith.

Never before did Judith doll herself up as she did for the personal meeting with Holofernes. She bathed, perfumed herself, coiffured her hair, and decked herself out with bracelets, earlets, rings, and other jewelry. "And the Lord also gave her more beauty: because all this dressing up did not proceed from sensuality, but from virtue. And therefore the Lord increased this her beauty, so that she appeared to all men's eyes incomparably lovely" (Jdt 10:4).

In Holofernes' Camp

Early morning, with her maid for a companion and a bag full of food and drink, she passed through the city gates and arrived at the enemy camp. The guards stopped her, then amazed at her message and beauty led her to their general. In the presence of Holofernes she employed all the wisdom and womanly cunning and courage at her command. She extolled Nebuchadnezzar and charmed Holofernes. She exposed the secret of Israelite weakness — "they have offended their God" (Jdt 11:9). Holofernes was trapped in the jaws of her wisdom and cunning.

Judith and her maid were given the freedom of the camp, to go and come as they pleased. They were permitted to eat their own food and thus escaped the obligation of taking pagan food that might be offered to idols. At nightfall Judith prayed for the success of her venture.

The fourth day she was invited to dine with Holofernes

and served herself and her maid the food and wine they
brought along. That evening the general, intoxicated with
her beauty and the wine, became drunk and fell into a
stupor. Then Judith put her maid on guard outside the
chamber door, tearfully and mumblingly begged the Lord
to help her. Holding the general's head up by the hair with
one hand, with the other she took his sword and in two
strokes lopped off his head. The headless body was rolled
away in a canopy. She called her maid and ordered her to
put the head into the empty food bag. Off they went to
Bethulia.

Reporting back at the city gates late at night, the townspeople were awakened and surprised to see her safe and
sound. Lights flickered in the dark, and in the silence of
the night Judith roused their drooping spirits and asked that
due credit be given to the Savior Lord: "Give all of you
glory to him, because he is good: because his mercy endureth
forever" (Jdt 13:21). Achior himself, when he saw the head
of Holofernes roll out in front of him, praised the God of
Israel and was converted.

Psychological Warfare

To put the enemy to rout, the Israelites resorted at sun-
rise to a psychological stratagem. They mustered themselves
and feigned an attack upon the Assyrians. With a lot of
noise and clamor they aroused the enemy, woke them up to
the fact of their general's death, and threw their army into
confusion. The Assyrians fled in all directions, taking off
through the fields and along hill paths, while the Israelites
gave them a merry chase.

To the conqueror Israel belonged the spoils. And to Judith
the people gave public acclaim. All the jewelry and finery
that belonged to Holofernes Judith offered as an everlasting
token of gratitude to the Lord. She did not want this
victory to be forgotten.

Her Last Days

St. Jerome, who freely translated the Book of Judith, wrote in his prologue: "Accept from my hand in the widowed Judith the perfect model of chastity." He sees chastity personified in her, cutting off the head of Lust. She controlled her body, beautiful though it was, with fasting, and putting aside her fashionable clothing again donned the robes of poverty.

The Book of Judith ends with her canticle to the Lord, an inspired song that résumés her heroic deed and begs all creatures to remain faithful to the Lord whom no one can resist. Judith lived virtuously to the ripe old age of a hundred and five years. Before her death she sets her maidservant free. She is buried alongside her husband in Bethulia.

Judith and Mary

Origen, the early Christian writer, exaggerates a bit when he describes Judith as "heroic in deeds, and of all women the most illustrious." That she was heroic in deeds there can be no doubt, but the most illustrious of all women was Mary the Mother of Jesus. Giving due credit to her, the Church in her liturgy recognizes Judith to be a forerunner of Mary. In Mary's two feasts, the Assumption and the Immaculate Conception, the liturgy applies Judith 15:10 to Mary: "Thou art the glory of Jerusalem, thou art the joy of Israel, thou art the honour of our people."

Both women, Judith and Mary, were willing to expose themselves to great suffering. In the encounter of the powers of good and evil, both were at hand to lend assistance and help rescue their people.

Both women seem to be so closely associated with their people that they typify the people of God, the Old Israel and the New. Judith sang in her canticle, "[The Assyrian] bragged that he would set my borders on fire, and kill my young men with the sword: to make my infants a prey, and my virgins captives" (Jdt 16:6). She identifies herself with Israel in this passage, just as in Chapter 12 of the Apocalypse Mary is identified with the Church. Yes, the more holy a woman is, the more woman she is — and the holier her progeny.

XI

The Confessions of Jeremiah

In the Sistine Chapel, in one fresco, the artist Michelangelo depicted an ancient prophet suffering and mournful. The prophet is seated, slightly stooped over, his head supported by his right hand. His hair and beard are disheveled, his forehead wrinkled, his eyes cast down. He seems to be looking down at blood and ruins. That ancient prophet is Jeremiah, the prophet of doom. It is his life and teaching that I should like to present now.

The Young Prophet

Jeremiah's hometown was Anathoth, a little town about three and a half miles northeast of Jerusalem. He was born there about 645 B.C., and belonged to the tribe of Benjamin (one of the twelve sons of the patriarch Jacob). He was in his early twenties when the Lord's call came to him that he should prophesy: "I know not how to speak," he answered, "I am too young" (1:6). Josiah, about the same age as Jeremiah, was king of Judah at the time.

As so many of the prophets preceding him — e.g., Moses and Isaiah — he shied away from the job. He was a shy lad, sensitive, warm and emotional, tenderhearted. "I did not sit celebrating in the circle of merrymakers; under the weight of your hand [God's hand] I sat alone because you filled me with indignation" (15:17). He pleaded with the Lord that he was too young and that he lacked the powers of expression befitting a prophet.

But the Lord called him anyway. "For it is I this day who have made you a fortified city, a pillar of iron, a wall of brass, against the whole land" (1:18). What was particularly distasteful to him was that he had to predict doom and destruction. His message was not cheerful but gloomy: "Whenever I speak, I must cry out, violence and outrage is my message" (20:8). He had a sympathetic heart but was driven to scold and reproach and threaten. No wonder we have adopted into our English language the word "jeremiad" — "a tale of woe."

The Political Problem

Jeremiah faced two conflicts in his life, one outward and the other inward. It was the outward conflict, mostly political and religious, which contributed to his inward troubles. Earlier in this series of biblical personalities, we noted that the people of God who stemmed from Abraham, who had been united into a kingdom by David, fell apart into a northern and southern kingdom — Israel in the north and Judah in the south. The split naturally weakened the nation. The year 721 marked the defeat of the northern kingdom of Israel at the hands of the Assyrians. Jeremiah came upon the scene when the same fate was about to befall the southern kingdom. Judah was to be devoured by the Babylonians, that people who lived at the easternmost tip of the Fertile Crescent. Jeremiah was torn between the love of his country and countrymen and duty to the Lord. He was squeezed in the vise of a political and religious conflict.

Palestine itself lay in between two great powers, the Babylonian on the Euphrates River and the Egyptian on the Nile.

The population was tugged at by two factions, pro-Babylonian and pro-Egyptian. Remotely we can compare the political situation at that time with our own, though we are a very much larger nation than Judah was. We are set between two powerful nations, the Chinese and the Russians — both Communist. We can be swallowed up by both or either of the two. At the same time within our borders we are struggling in a moral and religious crisis — divorce, delinquency, tension between labor and capital, religious formalism, sexuality, the racial problem, clericalism, etc. There is the further question whether we need a prophet or two of Jeremiah's caliber to reproach us today.

Judah was confronted with two enemies from without and an enemy from within — a fifth column. Jeremiah advocated that the Judeans who were given to the practice of idolatry, who worshiped the sun-god, wooden pillars, Baal — the pagan god of crops and herds, who sacrificed children to Molech, should revive the worship of the one true God. So he advised political neutrality on the one hand and religious revival on the other.

The Siege of 587

Through his prophetic eye he foresaw that because the worship in the temple at Jerusalem was a mere formality, that temple would fall and the city would be destroyed. He had much respect for the Jerusalem temple and its worship, yet he had to foretell its destruction and the end of its worship. By a sad coincidence, it was his custom to preach at the temple or the temple gate (7:2), at the very scene of disaster.

The disaster actually occurred in 587 B.C. The Babylonian king Nebuchadnezzar won against the Egyptians (after they had fought it out with and been weakened by the Assyrians) at Charchemish in 605, and from then on he had a clear path to the destruction of the temple and city of Jerusalem.

When the siege was on, Jeremiah was imprisoned for advising the Judean soldiers to quit fighting. He was a scapegoat, an outcast from his family, a traitor to his nation.

His plan was to let the Judeans go to Babylon, settle, flourish, and multiply there. He promised them that after 70 years they would be able to return to their homeland. He was so certain of the eventual outcome that he bought himself a plot of land at his birthplace, Anathoth. The Judeans were unconvinced.

What followed was the Babylonian Captivity, an exile lasting about 40 years — 587 to 538 B.C. The conqueror introduced a new military policy designed to snuff out nationalism and keep captive nations firmly under control. The new policy was quite different from what the Hebrews once practiced, that of extermination. It was to exile them from their native land to foreign soil. Foreign colonists then moved in to resettle the Judean countryside and incorporate it. The new policy thus was a case of severe exploitation and imperialism. Israel and Judah, a small divided nation, tasted the bitter lesson of exile.

It is estimated that 30,000 Judeans were deported to Babylon and lived in exile there. The whole catastrophe had been announced by Jeremiah beforehand. He preached repentance almost to the point of monotony, telling the people that the punishment resulted directly from their guilt. To lend force to his words, he himself remained a celibate, the first explicitly known in sacred history, never marrying because he did not want to rear a family of children who would die by the sword or be put into Babylonian slavery (cf. 16:1–4), as Christians are dragged into slave camps in our day. Jeremiah — about 60 years of age — chose to stay behind in Judah until later when he was abducted into Egypt by a pro-Egyptian party of Judeans and martyred there, probably stoned to death. His forty years of prophecy came to a tragic conclusion.

Read the first chapter of the Lamentations (attributed to

Jeremiah) to see how he felt about the fall of Jerusalem and the captivity. Like Christ he wept over the city, that city of David once converted into the city of God but which, like an unfaithful bride, proved herself unfaithful to her Divine Bridegroom. "How lonely she is now, the once crowded city. . . . Bitterly she weeps at night, tears upon her cheeks, with not one to console her. . . . Judah has fled into exile from oppression and cruel slavery. . . . The Lord has punished her for her many sins. . . . Look, O Lord, and see how worthless I have become. . . . Come, all you who pass by the way, look and see whether there is any suffering like my suffering which has been dealt me when the Lord afflicted me on the day of his blazing wrath. . . . The Lord is just; I had defied his command."

Radical Reform

What Jeremiah felt more keenly than national revolt was his inward conflict. His writing was the most autobiographical of all the literary prophets. Late in his prophetical life he called in Baruch, the scroll writer, to have him take dictation. When King Joakim, son of Josiah, had pieces of the dictation read to him, he angrily sliced off each piece as it was read and threw it into a flaming brazier, forcing Jeremiah to redo his work.

In his writings we catch glimpses of the prophet's inner life — how he was divided betwen loyalty to God and sympathy with his people, how he experienced sad trial when his countrymen turned against him, when he cursed his enemies and the day of his birth. His agony likens him to the Lamb of God who embodied in His own flesh and blood the messianic prophesy, "Yet I, like a trusting lamb led to slaughter, had not realized that they were hatching plots against me" (11:19).

His human effort failed, his heartfelt desires were unfulfilled. He kept urging his people to repair their ways and turn back to the worship of and obedience to the Lord: "Stand beside the earliest roads, ask the pathways of old which is the way to good, and walk it; thus you will find rest for your souls. But they said, 'We will not walk it' " (6:16).

He admitted that they were so far gone in their evil that they would not convert. "Can the Ethiopian change his skin? the leopard his spots? As easily would you be able to do good, accustomed to evil as you are" (13:23). What mental anguish must Jeremiah have experienced seeing his fellowmen on the road to perdition while he could not prevent them. Yet when he predicted punishment for them, in the same breath he prayed for them: "Even though our crimes bear witness against us, take action, O Lord, for the honor of your name — even though our rebellions are many, though we have sinned against you. O Hope of Israel, O Lord, our savior in time of need" (14:7–8). So many are the insights into the character of Jeremiah that bits of his writing have come to be called "The Confessions of Jeremiah." Look into Chapters 11, 12, 14, 15, 17, 18, 20.

St. Jerome calls the style of Jeremiah "simple and easy, most profound in majesty of thought." He writes in both poetry and prose. His style is jerky, full of disjointed sentences, as repetitious as would be the style of a sufferer who appeals to the Lord for help. The drama of his life, told so autobiographically, is a prelude to the *Confessions* of St. Augustine.

When reading his book, one should remember that it is divided into two parts, Chapters 1 to 45, and 46 to the end. The first part deals with his warnings to Judah, the second with threats against pagan nations, nine in all.

A Message of Hope

Jeremiah has two outstanding passages in his writings, outstanding because they are filled with promise and hope. The one is of the Messiah to come, the other of His kingdom.

"How long will you continue to stray, rebellious daughter? The Lord has created a new thing upon the earth: the woman must encompass the man with devotion" (31:22). What was "the new thing" to be? Did it simply mean that Israel or the remnant of it, that group of the poor and the devout who would welcome Christ into the world, would replace the old Israel? Or did it mean that a Messiah was to be born of a virgin? Both meanings could apply, the second in a fuller sense, and this is the sense in which St. Jerome accepts the passage. The "new thing" is a woman, Mary, who will encompass Christ within her womb.

The second prediction concerns Christ's spiritual kingdom, the Church. "Thus says the Lord: If you can break my covenant with day, and my covenant with night, so that day and night no longer alternate in sequence, then can my covenant with my servant David also be broken, so that he will not have a son to be king upon his throne, and my covenant with the priests of Levi who minister to me. Like the host of heaven which cannot be numbered, and the sands of the sea which cannot be counted, I will multiply the descendants of my servant David and the Levites who minister to me" (33:19–22). The second David is Jesus, and the host of heaven are the members called into His Church.

"The days are coming, says the Lord, when I will make a new covenant with the house of Israel and the house of Judah. It will not be like the covenant I made with their fathers the day I took them by the hand to lead them forth from the land of Egypt; for they broke my covenant, and I had to show myself their master, says the Lord. But this is the covenant which I will make with the house of Israel after those days, says the Lord. I will place my law within them, and write it upon their hearts: I will be their God, and they shall be my people" (31:31–33). Here we have the great promise, the great covenant of love which God would have with us, His people. It is enacted by the Holy Spirit in the Christ who is the covenant of the new law and the Spirit.

In Chapter 24, verse 7, the Lord's words are clearer and more to the point: "I will give them a heart with which to understand that I am the Lord. They shall be my people and I will be their God, for they shall return to me with their whole heart."

Practice Without Faith

It was not easy for Jeremiah to teach the people that God out of love made them to suffer for their sins — "with age-old love I have loved you; so I have kept my mercy toward you" (31:3). Yahweh was sending temporal punishment upon them to awaken them to their duty of love and service. Religious practice was so neglected that Josiah wept when the law of Moses, the Torah, was discovered accidentally in a rubbish pile that workmen were cleaning out of the Jerusalem temple. The discovery, however, gave Josiah the opportunity to sponsor the publication of the Torah and to teach Israel again the good news of what Yahweh had done for them and what his demands were.

Outwardly the people were paying homage to God in the temple, but their worship was only formal, external, and empty. Of what benefit was the written law, if they put no spirit into its observance. "How can you say, 'We are wise, we have the law of the Lord?' Why, that has been changed into falsehood by the lying pen of the scribes!" (8:8.) They were not rendering to the Lord the worship of their hearts. They were unfaithful to Him in the depth of their life. Outwardly they asked for pity and mercy, but inwardly they were still rebellious. Sin had an interiority, and if they were to be rid of it, they had to eliminate it by the roots. At heart the people were still crying against the Lord, "I will not serve" (2:20).

A Religion of the Heart

In Jeremiah faith meant abandonment to the will of the Lord. "What do you see, Jeremiah?" (1:11) was the question put to him in his personal experience of an encounter with Yahweh. Jeremiah would have us believe that God is the God of the heart of man, a personal God. In this teaching he strikes an original note in the Old Testament. God knows each one of us, all that we are and feel and suffer. We can confide in Him, and in Him we find sweet consolation in times of sorrow. Jeremiah did not merely preach this doctrine; he lived it. God demands man's heart in order to make it into a new heart.

He wants a purification of the heart, an interior change. "Cleanse your heart of evil, O Jerusalem, that you may be saved" (4:14). "I, the Lord, alone probe the mind and test the heart, to reward everyone according to his ways" (17:10). Man with his perverse heart cannot bring about this change of heart, but God can and will. Such is his promise in the covenant of love: "I will give them a heart with which to understand that I am the Lord" (24:7).

At times we feel disappointment and loneliness because after many attempts to do the will of God we still find no change of heart. Jeremiah too felt himself unsuited for his duty, the task of prophecy, but he turned to Yahweh for strength. Throughout his cloudy and gloomy message there streaks a ray of hope and faith and courage which God vouched to him: "I am with you to deliver you" (1:19). Jeremiah found joy in proclaiming God's word: "When I found your words, I devoured them; they became my joy and the happiness of my heart" (15:16).

XII

Ezekiel in Exile

STORM wind. Cloud. Lightning. Four-faced and four-winged creatures. Sparkling wheels within wheels. A crystallike firmament. Above the firmament a throne with one seated "who had the appearance of a man" (Ezek 1:26). "Such was the vision of the likeness of the glory of the Lord" (Ezek 1:28). This is no description of a nightmare but an introductory picture of the visions which came to the prophet Ezekiel. No fantasy, no matter how fantastic, can visualize for us the majesty of God.

Judging from the strong and wild imaginings to be read in his book, one would say Ezekiel was a man of unusual temperament — sometimes harsh and insistent. Once he began to prophesy, he had many, many prophetic visions. To us his visions seem outlandish. Some scholars have thought — but wrongly — that he had an abnormal psychology, was the victim of hallucinations, had impaired speech (aphasia) and muscular seizures (catalepsy). But strong-minded as he was, as were the prophets preceding him, he had no fear of man in prophesying for Yahweh. His duty was to carry the prophetic spirit beyond Israel's borders, and to show the people that the Lord's influence extends to all sectors of the world.

Ezekiel was a prophet-priest; he had that double calling from Yahweh. Of the three special vocations in the old covenant, priest, prophet, and king, Ezekiel lacked only the latter. In an audio-visual way we are informed about his calling: "The Lord God said to me: Son of man, eat what is before you; eat this scroll, then go, speak to the house of Israel. . . . I ate it, and it was as sweet as honey in my mouth" (Ezek 3:1, 3). He was saying that Yahweh's words were tasty to one who welcomed and received them.

We do not know much about the man himself, because he is not nearly so autobiographical as his contemporary Jeremiah. His one and only book is not informative about himself or his surroundings. He appears to have been a simple, earnest fellow who drove a point home by repetition. His name means "God is strong" or "God strengthens." He was about thirty years old when he began to prophesy — about the same age Christ was at the start of His public life. His prophetic career began in 593 B.C. and lasted about a quarter century. While Jeremiah stayed behind in Palestine, Ezekiel was a prophet in exile.

Under the Babylonian king Nebuchadnezzar, Ezekiel's compatriots were deported in 597 and 587 B.C. to Babylonia, a world power on the Tigris and Euphrates rivers. Our prophet was the first of his kind to receive the prophetic call outside of Palestine — in a pagan land. Because of his self-effacing silence, we cannot reconstruct his life or give details of his birth and death. At any rate, we know he was never to return to Jerusalem even if he had grandiose visions of the city and temple rebuilding.

At first he feels, as so many do in their apostolate, that without the Lord's help he is unable to prophesy. Ninety times or so in his book he refers to himself as "son of man," which implies man with his innate weakness, his littleness in contrast to God's greatness. By one figure of speech after another he lets us know that Yahweh alone endows him with the ability to speak out to his fellowmen. His tongue sticks to his palate, he is bound with cords, he has to lie on his left then on his right side for long periods, he has to prepare his own food. All such hardships are indications that Yahweh has control of Ezekiel and wants to restrict his use of prophecy.

Ezekiel does not immediately see the fruits of his labors. His mission is to sow the word of the Lord, but the Lord Himself is to take the harvest. We are reminded by this detail of his life that apostolic good can lie fallow seemingly for years, beyond the lifetime of an apostle.

Ezekiel had so profound and lasting an influence on Jewish doctrine and worship that he has been titled the "Father of Judaism." His emphatic teaching on the exodus recalled the pivotal event of all Hebrew history. "Thus speaks the Lord God: The day I chose Israel, I swore to the descendants of the house of Jacob; in the land of Egypt I revealed myself to them and swore: I am the Lord, your God. That day I swore to bring them out of the land of Egypt to the land I had scouted for them, a land flowing with milk and honey, a jewel among all lands" (Ezek 20:5–6). Whatever were his hard sayings to his exiled countrymen, they all reflect to the exodus event.

A City Under Siege

When Jerusalem was set afire in 587, and his prophecy was fulfilled, Ezekiel was vindicated before his countrymen. Displaced in a foreign land and bereaved of his wife, he was told by the Lord not to mourn over her. Mourning would have symbolized the Hebrew lament over the fall of Jerusalem, which in itself was a good riddance.

At first the Judeans falsely hoped God would never permit the city and temple to be destroyed. Would He ever allow the temple of His presence to go to ruin? They were rumored to be saying about the prophet, "The vision he sees is a long way off; he prophesies of the distant future" (Ezek

12:27). With all his might Ezekiel fought against their false hope and Jewish complacency. His repeated warning finds an echo in the outspoken men, today's prophets, who warn the American nation that unless it is strong spiritually, it will fall victim to hostile foreign power.

What a dismal picture the prophet sketches of Jerusalem a decade before its destruction! Crimes abound. Idolatry, murder, theft, robbery, adultery, incest, perjury, oppression of the poor and orphan and widow. The account reads very much like the front page of a modern newspaper. Jerusalem is a bloody gangland, "a reproach and an object of scorn, a terrible warning to the nations . . ." (Ezek 5:15). The prophet can find no viler term of comparison for her than "harlot"!

Ezekiel is never so vehement nor so flamboyant in his speech as when he speaks about Israel's harlotry (Chapter 16). Yahweh picks up Israel as an orphan in the land of Canaan. She is unkempt, unfed. He has compassion on her, takes care of her, and watches her grow up into a marriageable woman "old enough for love." "So I spread the corner of my cloak over you to cover your nakedness," signifying his intention to enter into a marriage covenant with her. He clothes and decorates and feasts her. "You were exceedingly beautiful, with the dignity of a queen. You were renowned among the nations for your beauty, perfect as it was, because of my splendor which I had bestowed on you."

"But you were captivated by your own beauty, you used your renown to make yourself a harlot, and you lavished your harlotry on every passerby, whose own you became." Ezekiel plays upon the idea that harlotry is synonymous with the idolatry the Israelites learn from their pagan neighbors. From them they adopt the practice of human sacrifice — "sons and daughters you had borne me you took and offered as sacrifices to be devoured by them." To try to win favor with the gods of fertility, they even resort to ritual prostitution — "you raised

for yourself a platform and a dais in every public place."
Rather than take payment for its harlotry, Israel consorts with
paganism and gives payment.

The Lord looks among the Judeans for someone to stem
the tide of her crime, to balance the evil with some good,
but He discovers no one. "Therefore I have poured out my
fury upon them; with my fiery wrath I have consumed them;
I have brought down their conduct upon their heads" (Ezek
22:31).

Judean Misconceptions

Ezekiel's task was made all the more difficult because of
three wrong impressions the Hebrews had. They did not
think the fall of Judah and Jerusalem possible: God was on
their side and He would prevent it. How mistaken they
were! Archaeology has revealed the extent of the devastation
wrought by the Babylonians on Palestine. Their destruction
was drastic and terrible. They practically leveled the city.
Several centuries passed before the countryside returned to
normalcy.

The Israelites presumed too that their Babylonian captivity
would be brief. Yahweh would see to their speedy return to
the homeland. In reality, they were kept homeless for half a
century, from 587 to 538 B.C.

Although Ezekiel is reticent about their actual condition
in Babylonia, the deportees were not as uncomfortable as
King Nebuchadnezzar might have made them. They did suffer the hardships of the deportation — some died on the way.
But after arriving in Babylon and setting to work in the cities,
on construction jobs and running businesses, or farming on
better land than they had known in Palestine, they enjoyed
a semifreedom. They gained economically. They were permitted to retain family ties and often housed together in
neighborhoods where they felt few pangs of homesickness.
Spiritually they suffered most, because they were far from

Yahweh's land, where they could offer sacrifice to Him in the temple. Ezekiel pinned his hopes for the restoration of Israel on his fellow exiles, and not on the folks back home.

The third wrong impression the Judeans labored under, though it was only partially wrong, was that they were unjustly punished for ancestral sins: they were victims of national responsibility. They, the children, had to pay the penalty for their parents. God was unjust and unholy toward them. Their resentment no doubt sprang from the longstanding notion among them that as a group they were guilty for past sins. To their credit they were nationalistic. They had the strong group spirit of the one for the many and the many for the one. As a group they had to bear responsibility for good and evil. Corporate guilt and corporate responsibility. They coined a proverb to express their popular feeling: "Fathers have eaten green grapes, thus their children's teeth are on edge" (Ezek 18:2). Even if they had been betrayed by their elders, they were wrong in disclaiming any guilt of their own.

From Presumption to Despair

As long as the exiles were not brought news about the fall of their city and country, they continued to presume upon God's mercy. The longer the exile lasted, the more easily did their feelings swing from presumption to despair. So Ezekiel accused them first of their sins and insisted on divine retribution, and then later he began to preach mercy to keep them from despair.

Away from the Jerusalem temple and worship, the people were tempted to idolatry and drifted into pagan ways. No crime was so abominable in all Israelitic history, even in their own estimation, as idolatry. The people thought God had abandoned them. Ezekiel had to issue warnings against their worshiping pagan Babylonian gods who, so it seemed, were victorious over Yahweh.

At this stage of the exile, when the people floundered from optimism to pessimism, Ezekiel began to change his tune. Formerly he predicted the fall in terms of the Lord's punishing a sinful people (Chapters 1–24). Now he held out to them a prospect of hope (Chapters 33–48). He buoyed up their spirits with the promise of a future messianic king and kingdom. "As for you, son of man, speak to the house of Israel: You people say, 'Our crimes and our sins weigh us down; we are rotting away because of them. How can we survive?' Answer them: As I live, says the Lord God, I swear I take no pleasure in the death of the wicked man, but rather in the wicked man's conversion, that he may live. Turn, turn from your evil ways: Why should you die, O house of Israel?" (Ezek 33:10–11.)

One of the exiled prophet's favorite themes is the announcement of a shepherd-king who will deliver his people from captivity. He quotes the Lord: "I will appoint one shepherd over them to pasture them, my servant David; he shall pasture them and be their shepherd. I, the Lord, will be their God, and my servant David shall be prince among them. I, the Lord, have spoken" (Ezek 34:23–24).

You may ask, how does King David, deceased centuries before, get into the picture? You see, in uttering prophecies, Ezekiel had to use a sort of double-talk. To deal with the situation at hand, he resorted to contemporary and past history for realistic background to his prophecy. Consequently he lost sight of chronological perspective, bringing bits of real history together into a kaleidoscopic view.

The exiles were promised a return to their native country and the restoration of their nation — a new kingdom, a new Israel (which was accomplished in the kingdom of the Church). Eventually the national and secular kingdom would give way to a universal and spiritual kingdom. In Chapter 11:16–17 Ezekiel instills new hope and heart in the people, and in Chapter 37 he continues his prediction.

The Valley of Dry Bones

In this latter chapter he describes his vision of the plain of dry bones and their dramatic return to life. That vision has been set to music in the moving Negro spiritual *Dry Bones.* "Ezekiel cried: Dem dry bones, dem dry bones, dem dry bones. Now hear the word of the Lord. Ezekiel connecta dem dry bones — toe bone, foot bone, heel bone, ankle bone, leg, knee. Dem bones, dem bones gonna walk aroun'." Using the figure of the resurrection of the dead, the songwriter is able to portray the restoration of Israel. The bones represent God's people who resurrect into the new Israel. Moreover, two sticks are joined together to symbolize the reunion of Judah and Israel under a messianic king.

The Messiah is, by a figure of speech, a sprout of the dried-up tree of David shooting forth new growth. He is a good shepherd in contrast with the many bad shepherds in Israel's history. In the prophetic vision, merging present with past, David the shepherd is eclipsed by the Messiah.

Interior Renewal

At the same time that Ezekiel offers his people the possibility of a glorious future, he inculcates two moral lessons. He waxes eloquent about the need of interior religion. Religion must spring from within, from the heart, for then only is a sincere conversion to Yahweh possible. Ezekiel feels himself and the nation bound by an either-or decision: either convert wholeheartedly to Yahweh or abandon the idea of living under him. Yahweh is a jealous God who brooks no other gods before Him (cf. Ezek 39:25).

The temptation to shunt off responsibility and avert personal blame is quite human. But against the Israelite tendency to throw the blame upon their ancestors, Ezekiel preaches the duty of the person to the community. Each of the exiles is personally responsible: "Therefore I will judge you, house of Israel, each one according to his ways, says the Lord God"

(Ezek 18:30). God is just, and His justice will not punish the innocent along with the guilty.

If Ezekiel were living in our day and were to let his prophetic imagination roam over the human situation, would he cease to rant against evil and abuse? History repeats itself. World power, although it is no longer localized in Babylonia, is still an imminent evil. Daily we hear and read about threats and counterthreats which can evoke global destruction. Destruction is grown to a bigger scale; it is big enough now to engulf all of us. It hovers above us as a reminder that life on earth is an exile.

We are tempted too with modern idols of power and pleasure. Human sacrifice and temple prostitution — if they disgusted a prophet once upon a time, would they not draw down his wrath and scathing rebuke today, even though they have been brought out of the temple into the world scene?

What Ezekiel had to say about personal responsibility holds good for me and for all time. I cannot delegate anyone to shoulder my responsibility, because I myself am free and responsible. I have the care of my own conscience: "I must pay for my own sins, and I cannot borrow anyone else's absolution." I hear God's spokesman saying to me, "The virtuous man's virtue shall be his own, as the wicked man's wickedness shall be his" (Ezek 18:20).

The messianic kingdom which the prophet predicted is by no means over. The prospect of a new heaven and a new earth looms before us, and a happy kingdom that will have no end. Christ is the messianic King who is to return once and for all, in glory and majesty. He will again enflesh and enliven the dry bones of men, resurrecting them to life forever.

XIII

A Dialogue With Job

CHAPTER 28 of the Book of Job contains a poem on wisdom and, in part, catches the spirit of the whole book, whether an addition to the original or not. For Job is a piece of wisdom literature. Nowadays we still speak of a "sage" piece of advice, which usually comes from a wise man.

The Eastern sages were wise men, mostly teachers, who trained men for the civil service, and in the course of their teaching composed wise writings. King Solomon had such a reputation for wisdom that many books of the Old Testament were attributed to him, though he did not actually write them all. The main character in the Book of Job was evidently a wise and faithful man who was searching for the meaning of life, which was the main concern of all wisdom literature.

The Book of Job is a fairly long parable, a "comparison" story striking home a deeply felt human truth. Although the Hebrew sages sought wisdom wherever they could find it, and plumbed the human heart deeply, its longings and anxieties, they were well aware that real wisdom was a gift from God. Some of it could be acquired by a study of divine wisdom. When our Lord used the parable, as He so often did, He

was speaking in the tradition of Hebrew literature. Many of
His remarks as handed down to us are "wise sayings."

The Prose Section

The scene of our folk tale is laid on two levels, heaven
and earth. The action takes place in both spheres, but it
begins on earth. The locale, more precisely, is the borders of
the land of Edom or Arabia. The time is about 520 or fifth
century B.C., although there is much room for speculation
on this point. Anyway, the time is after the displacement or
exile of God's chosen people, the Israelites, to Babylonia. The
problem of suffering was vexing the Israelite nation. There
is another telltale mark about the time: there was consider-
able use of the Aramaic language during a transition period,
when Hebrew was gradually giving way to Aramaic, the language our Lord spoke.

The principal character of our folk tale is a bedouin sheik
named Job. Job is an upright and comparatively blameless
father of seven sons and three daughters. He is not only
saintly but wealthy. He has 7000 sheep, 3000 camels, 500
oxen, etc. According to our modern standards of living, we
might call him a gentleman farmer, rather well-to-do. When
we first meet him, he is enjoying health and prosperity. He
has the comfort of friendships.

The scene changes from earth to heaven. One day the
heavenly court assembles and Satan, not the evil spirit we
think of, but any opponent or instigator to evil, appears with
the group. God inquires where he hails from, and Satan, the
adversary, answers, "From roaming and patrolling the earth"
— to investigate mundane affairs. The Lord asks him if he
has seen Job, "there is no one on earth like him, blameless
and upright, fearing God and avoiding evil" (Job 1:8).

Satan replies that he has, but he attributes Job's piety to
his prosperity — the two so hinge together that if God would
permit him to destroy Job's prosperity, his piety would dis-

appear too. Job can afford to be pious as long as he is prosperous. But piety without prosperity is unthinkable to Satan. To prove His point against Satan, the Lord permits a series of calamities to befall Job, showing how willing He is to try Job.

First, robbers and plunderers rid Job of his oxen and camels. Along come lightning and a desert wind to destroy his sheep and ten children. His wife, seeing him unwilling to give an inch to Satan, for he will not complain against divine providence or call God unjust, is ready to desert him. Job feels the full brunt of the disaster, and still his patience does not run out: "The Lord gave and the Lord has taken away; blessed be the name of the Lord!" (Job 1:21.) His wife nags and taunts him: "Are you still holding to your innocence? Curse God and die." She gets the typical reply, "Are even you going to speak as senseless women do? We accept good things from God; and should we not accept evil?" (Job 2:9–10.)

Satan believes his wager with God is unfair; he is betting against too great odds. He is of the opinion Job has not been tested enough. God refused to let him lay hand on Job himself. The Lord then relents, and Satan afflicts Job with physical pain, so that there is nothing left of him but skin and bones. He has to sit upon a pile of refuse, a dung heap, scratching his sores and bewailing his lot.

Poetic Justice

After he suffers for months, three friends come to visit him, supposedly to console and comfort him. He is lonely, for suffering tends to exile him from his fellowmen. His friends hardly know what to think or say when they lay eyes on him. Instead of offering him solace in his misery, they begin to debate and reason with him. They engage in three full rounds of argument with him.

There must be some big flaw in his life. He must be guilty

of monstrous crime, for following the traditional line of
thinking, they see suffering — poverty, sickness, death — only
as the result of sin. Guilt and punishment are correlative.
Let Job repent and the Lord will restore him to his prosperity. The three friends, Eliphaz, Zophar, and Bildad present
the reverse side of the argument launched by Satan in
heaven. He joined prosperity to piety. They join punishment
with guilt. In their customary thinking there is no possibility
of innocent suffering.

We should not represent the three as coldhearted; they
simply are children of their day, no wiser than their generation. Eliphaz is the most personable of the three, a great
thinker, full and sure of his wisdom. He argues, "Is it because
of your piety that he reproves you — that he enters with you
into judgment? Is not your wickedness manifold? Are not
your iniquities endless?" (Job 22:4–5). Zophar is a tradi-
tionalist, a small, mean-minded old fellow who is steeped in
the past. "Do you not know this from olden time, since
man was placed upon the earth, that the triumph of the
wicked is short and the joy of the impious but for a moment?" (Job 20:4–5.) Bildad is the kind who stands for no
nonsense: "How long will you utter such things? The words
from your mouth are like a mighty wind!" (Job 8:2.)

All three argue that God has concern for human life,
awards good and punishes evil — the commonly accepted
principle of their day. So far there is nothing wrong in their
logic. But they extend their argument too far: all sufferers are
evildoers; Job is a sufferer, therefore he is an evildoer. A sinner because he is a sufferer. Thus they simply do not understand why the innocent should suffer, and that is why they
become more smug and severe toward Job as he insists upon
his innocence. Their argument follows the same pattern:
God is good, His government of the world is just, and Job's
suffering is an indication of his past sinful life. The argument
runs through three cycles: the three friends present a side,

Job has a reply, always maintaining himself innocent, and they repeat the procedure.

There is a marked contrast between the Job who begins and ends the folk tale and the Job who speaks up in righteous self-defense, especially in his conversation with God. The patience of Job wears thin as he flings defiant remarks at his persecutor. Innocent as he is, why should God take it out on him? The one who should really stand trial for responsibility and guilt is God. Job finds the divine presence overpowering, never letting him alone: "How long will it be before you look away from me, and let me alone long enough to swallow my spittle? Though I have sinned, what can I do to you, O watcher of men?" (Job 7:19–20.) God seems to be judging Job capriciously: "If it be a question of strength, he is mighty; and if of judgment, who will call him to account?" (Job 9:19.) The two, God and Job, are locked together in an uneven fight: "I am the prey," complains Job, "his wrath assails, he gnashes his teeth against me . . . he seized me by the neck and dashed me to pieces . . . he has set me up for a target; his arrows strike me from all directions . . . he pierces me with thrust upon thrust; he attacks me like a warrior" (Job 16:9–14).

Elihu, a character introduced later into the story by some anonymous writer, is an impetuous and impatient fellow who takes over where the three friends leave off. He is peeved at them because older and seemingly wiser they are unable to answer Job. He has nothing new to add, excepting perhaps to argue that not all suffering or misfortune is a punishment. It can be correctional too, forestalling man from his evil ways.

The Divine Defense

Chapters 38 and 39 of the Book of Job are devoted to the Lord's speech. The Lord speaks from a whirlwind or storm cloud, a familiar setting in the Old Testament for many of His theophanies. "Who is this," He asks, "that obscures divine plans with words of ignorance? Gird up your loins now, like a man; I will question you, and you tell me the answers!" (Job 38:2–3.)

The Lord's purpose is not to penetrate the mystery of suffering — to explain the *why* of it. He first points to the marvels of nature. The light, rain, snow, the full description of the heavens, then an enumeration of the animal world, particularly the crocodile and hippopotamus — are all meant to illustrate God's wisdom and power. They are contrasted with human ignorance and weakness. If man cannot understand the secrets of the world of nature, how can he with his puny mind hope to solve the riddle of suffering? How can he dare to criticize God's running of the universe? God's wisdom and power are to be seen in the design and fabric of His creation. God offers no positive, speculative solution to the problem of evil. He simply wants to teach Job humility. Job has to admit that there must be a wise but hidden purpose in allowing the innocent to suffer. Suffering, whatever purpose it has, has its origin in God: "He does great things past finding out, marvelous things beyond reckoning. Who can say to him, 'What are you doing?' " (Job 9:10, 12.)

Job confessed to his speaking out of turn, to lacking reverence in his language and finding fault with God's government of the universe. He felt bitter toward God when the pressure was on him, yet he never doubted or denied God's existence as some do who detect evil in the world. For him it was a question of God's character: Is God good or bad? When he "looked for good, then evil came." He had expected his virtue to guarantee him a life of peace and happiness. Death was to be the end of a serene old age.

Job's Repentance

What his friends miss in him, or rather fail to see, is the joy at the heart of Job's sorrow, the joy of his belief in the presence of God. Job strikes a happy note in saying, "But as

for me, I know that my Vindicator [Goel] lives" (Job 19:25).
God will avenge him somehow; for the present it does not
matter how.

Job is princely in his grief and in his founding of hope
upon faith. In a final address to the Lord he faces up to him
and admits his wrong: "I had heard of you by word of mouth,
but now my eye has seen you. Therefore I disown what I have
said, and repent in dust and ashes" (Job 42:5–6). Job is
first of all a man of faith who looks mystifiedly at God and
His ways. By blind faith he accepts God as He really is and
as He deals with the world and mankind. Whatever consolation Job feels is in the Divine Presence, that practical and
personal experience of God which is invaluable in any
situation.

The debate between God and Satan runs out, and Satan is
defeated, after the two agreed earlier that piety based only on
prosperity is shallow and insincere. The proper way to settle
the issue is to put Job to a test. There is no real, solid virtue
without a test. Throughout the trial it is the will of God
which must be done. Job has no selfish purpose undermining
his virtue, no greedy aim at a reward for himself. If he has,
his virtue will never be able to stand the strain. Virtue is
selfish that does not endure a test.

Job's story has a happy ending, but — what is more surprising — it ends happily in this life. For Christians that is
an unexpected ending, for ordinarily the faithful look for
a happy ending beyond the grave. God's people living under
the Old Testament had no clear concept of an afterlife. God
vindicates Himself in the present life of Job by restoring to
him a double share of his wealth. His wife returns, and
seven other sons and three daughters are born to them. In
this way God prepares the world for a fuller revelation: true
reward is not worldly prosperity but eternal life and enjoy-
ment in God's presence. The merit of Job is that he raises
the question of retribution for good and evil and gropes for

a solution beyond this earthly life. He takes a step in the right direction and leads finally — three centuries later — to the doctrine of retribution after death.

Job and Jesus

There is a theological if not historical link between Job sitting sorrowfully on the dung heap and Christ kneeling painfully in the garden of Gethsemane. Both feel the burden of suffering and loneliness. The one cries out, "Pity me, O you my friends, for the hand of God has struck me!" (Job 19:21.) The other utters the lament, "My soul is sad, even unto death. Wait here and watch with me" (Mt 26:38). The Redeemer hanging upon the cross, as Job perched on the dunghill, feels keenly the desertion by friends. But there is no defiant tone in that mysterious cry from the cross, "My God, my God, why hast thou forsaken me?" (Mt 27:46.) It is in the suffering Servant that the Christian discovers the full mystery of evil; suffering befalls not man alone but the God-man.

We have all met the child who suffers abandonment by its parents, the sick abed who have no visitors and are lonely, the aged who outlived their generation and are cast aside by relatives and friends. They can sympathize with Job and Jesus. The arms of the cross are stretched out to embrace them all. They beckon and invite, "If anyone wishes to come after me, let him deny himself, and take up his cross, and follow me" (Mt 16:24).

The Mystery of Suffering

Job is any man and every man in pain who asks himself, "What is the meaning and value of my life? Why must I sooner or later en route meet with suffering?" In Job we have an example of a man who refutes the ancient idea that suffering is necessarily due to sin. On the other hand, he defends God against any accusations of injustice or lack of wisdom and power. Ultimately he is right in giving no definitive solution to the mystery of suffering. God's motive in permitting pain ends in mystery.

There comes a harvesttime, however, when patient suffering will have its reward. "Behold, the farmer [Job was a gentleman farmer] waits for the precious fruit of the earth, being patient until it receives the early and late rain. Do you also be patient; strengthen your hearts; for the coming of the Lord is at hand. . . . You have heard of the patience of Job, and you have seen the purpose of the Lord, how the Lord is merciful and compassionate" (Jas 5:7–8, 11).

XIV

Daniel, His Dreams and Visions

WE RENEW our acquaintance with Daniel annually on the last Sunday of Pentecost when the dark and mysterious passage of Matthew 24:15–35 is read to us in the liturgy. The passage begins very forebodingly: "Therefore when you see the abomination of desolation, which was spoken of by Daniel the prophet . . ."

Has it ever struck you — it has me, because I have been asked about it more than once — how ominous the "abomination of desolation" sounds? The words are almost onomatopoeic; without knowing their real meaning one can imagine walls crashing down or an army crushing its foe. But to get at the meaning of the phrase, we will have to turn to the story of Daniel.

Daniel was a young Hebrew, probably between 12 and 15 years of age, when he was taken captive and deported to Babylon in 605 B.C. He joined a group of young men as a page to be educated for three years in the royal court of Nebuchadnezzar. They were young men "without any defect, handsome, intelligent and wise, quick to learn, and prudent in judgment" (Dan 1:4). Daniel was drafted into the group because he was either born of royal blood or, what is more likely, belonged to some noble family. He was cut out to be a statesman and hence was pressed into the king's service. This happened at a time when kings were notorious for doing "evil before the Lord" (2 Kings 23:32), which meant that they usurped Yahweh's power and lured His people away from Him.

In the City of Babylon

What sort of city was Babylon? It was Nebuchadnezzar's pride and joy; he built it. Built very much like a medieval city, it was square-shaped, had huge walls surrounding it, with a moat deep and wide, the better to ward off enemy attack. The walls were so broad that a street large enough for four-horse chariots ran on top of it. The street was flanked by rows of buildings. The city contained the hanging gardens, one of the seven wonders of the world which the king constructed for his Persian wife and queen. She was used to mountainous territory and could look out at artificial tree-covered mountains. How wide-eyed the Hebrews must have been at their arrival in this magnificent place!

If Daniel arrived in Babylon in 605 B.C. and was still in the royal service when the empire fell to the Persian King Cyrus in 539, then we can readily reckon that he was a public servant for over sixty years, having served under four kings. It is no wonder his name, as we shall see from the important counsels and decisions he handed down, was traditionally associated with wisdom. His contemporary Ezekiel ironically prophesied to one foreign ruler, "Oh yes, you are wiser than Daniel" (28:3). Ezekiel may have had back in his mind the thought of an earlier Daniel who was reputed among the fifteenth-century Canaanites for his wisdom, but in any case the practical good judgment of a Daniel was proverbial.

The Book of Daniel

Daniel could make little or no claim to be God's spokesman, a prophet, for he did not address himself to Israel. He did have something important to say to the Gentile kings whom he served. His message is unique in this, that he directed it not to Israel but to her captors, while the prophet Ezekiel tended to the exiles themselves.

The sixth-century Daniel with whom the Book of Daniel begins, is the hero but not the author of the book. The latter is unknown. The book was edited and reedited so that it swept through sacred history from the sixth to the second century before Christ. Its division into three parts, Chapters 1–6, 7–12, 13–14 (an appendix), the use of three languages, Aramaic, Hebrew and Greek, and the style itself, now give evidence that more than one author took part in its composition. The ghost-writer in the second century, whoever he was, drew from oral and written tradition to build up his hero and make a telling comparison between his day of persecution and the past. He exhorted his countrymen to withstand persecution as the Hebrews of old did for the sake of their faith.

In the Royal Court

The young Daniel at court sets the standard for Hebrew conduct in pagan surroundings by refusing to touch food prohibited by Jewish dietary laws and asking for vegetables and water instead. It is interesting to note how the number "ten" figures in this early incident of his life. After ten days, he and his three friends "look healthier and better fed than any of the young men who ate from the royal table" (Dan 1:15). And once they finish with their apprenticeship, in their wisdom and prudence they are "ten times better than all the magicians and enchanters" in the king's service.

Whenever it was, King Nebuchadnezzar had a dream which gave him insomnia. So he called upon his wise men not only to explain the dream but to read his mind and spell out the dream. The wise men, even at the threat of death, unanimously declared themselves incapable and the gods alone equal to it. Seeing himself liable to die along with the wise men, Daniel hurried home to inform the trio about their impending doom. They prayed God during the night to reveal the mystery of the dream.

Daniel then asked to be brought to the king. What the king had seen in his dream was a statue made of gold, silver, bronze, and iron. A mountain stone came tumbling down and crushed the statue. The stone expanded almost like volcanic rock to cover the whole earth. So much for the dream itself.

Immediately Daniel set to work divulging its meaning to the king. The four metals symbolized four kingdoms, empires, which were to topple in succession. The king's empire was to be the first to fall. Daniel's prediction (or was it some editor's hindsight?) had great perspective: it saw the Babylonian (gold), Median (silver), Persian (bronze), and Greek-Syrian (iron) empires give way to the eternal messianic kingdom (the stone). Four centuries at least would have to pass before the divine plan was ready for execution. A period of persecution would precede the last and eternal kingdom: "The God of heaven will set up a kingdom that shall never be destroyed or delivered up to another people; rather, it shall break in pieces all these kingdoms and put an end to them, and it shall stand forever" (Dan 2:44).

A wild flight of the imagination, you say? Not so wild when we visualize the rolling mountainous terrain of the Near East. The same imagery was employed by Christ when he reminded contemporary Hebrew leaders of what would happen if they rejected him. "Everyone who falls upon that stone [Christ] will be broken to pieces; but upon whomever it falls, it will grind him to powder" (Lk 20:18).

Apocalyptic Writing

Anyone who picks up the Book of Daniel to read may be tempted at this point to lay it aside. What should one make of this crazy-quilt pattern of his thought? Perhaps too many editors dipped their quills into murky ink and botched the original work? There are definitely midrashic and apocalyptic elements in the book, but they combine to add emphasis to the theme of its teaching.

Apocalyptic literature grew in a period of crisis for the Hebrew faith, while the Hebrews despite suffering and persecution were coaxed into trusting in final victory under Yahweh. As we saw in part already, this type of literature was characterized by highly imaginative descriptions, the use of symbolic numbers, names, beasts, and earth disturbances. Daniel was featured in one predicament after another, yet Yahweh never failed to rescue him.

The kings of pagan nations never seemed to learn that they were instruments in God's hands. Their thrones were theirs only because God wanted to use them as whips to chastise his people Israel.

More Royal Dreams

The story continues in the first person, with Nebuchadnezzar writing his people a letter and narrating a second dream. "It has seemed good to me to publish the signs and wonders which the most high God has accomplished in my regard" (Dan 3:99). He describes a tall, magnificent tree, centered in the earth, whose branches are fruitbearing and cast a shadow over the whole earth. A holy sentinel — angel — is given orders by the most high God to cut the tree down. Only its stump is to be left, and that stump, by means of personification, turns into Nebuchadnezzar himself. "You are that tree, O king, large and strong!" interprets Daniel. The king is to be stricken with lycanthropy, a form of insanity in which he supposedly prowls the earth like a wolf. He is told by Daniel that the kingdom will be preserved for him "once you have learned it is heaven that rules" (Dan 4:23). The king may not have been Nebuchadnezzar himself but a successor who, records show, secluded himself in an Arabian desert for seven years. The factual history is unimportant; what is relevant is that proud kings are taught a lesson in humility: those who walk in pride the King of heaven is able to humble (Dan 4:34).

A third king who calls upon Daniel for an interpretation is King Belshazzar. He and his court are in the midst of a banquet, regaling themselves, when suddenly they are startled by the sight of a hand appearing and writing on a plaster wall. The spectacle unnerves the king; his face blanches, his hip joints shake, and his knees knock (cf. Dan 5:6). His wise men can give him no answer, and again his face grows pale and his lords are thrown into confusion (cf. Dan 5:9). The queen puts his mind to rest by telling him about Daniel, "in whom is the spirit of the holy God," and who is seen "to have brilliant knowledge and godlike wisdom" (Dan 5:11).

What is the meaning of this script? the king asks Daniel, and offers him a third-ranking position in his kingdom for an answer. Daniel refuses the offer but volunteers the solution to the handwriting. In the same way as the kings preceding him, Belshazzar has lost favor with God for misusing royal power. His kingship is due to end and will be divided and taken over by the Medes and Persians.

In the Lions' Den

There is some doubt about who the next king was under whom Daniel served, whether he was Darius the Mede or Cyrus the Persian. In any case, men who were politically jealous of him trumped up a law by which all citizens, including Daniel, had to pray to no one but the king for thirty days. Daniel paid no attention to the law but "continued his custom of going home to kneel in prayer and give thanks to his God in the upper chamber three times a day, with the windows open toward Jerusalem" (Dan 6:11).

That is how he was found praying. When the men dragged

him off to the king, the latter was sorry he had to enforce the law. He had to order Daniel to be cast into the lions' den, not however without expressing the wish, "May your God, whom you serve so constantly, save you" (Dan 6:17).

Daniel sat among the lions unharmed. Then the king reserved places for the politicians and their families among the lions, and he issued a new decree demanding reverence and fear of the God of Daniel. "For he is the living God, enduring forever; his kingdom shall not be destroyed, and his dominion shall be without end. He is a deliverer and savior, working signs and wonders in heaven and on earth, and he delivered Daniel from the lions' power" (Dan 6:27–28).

To avoid some repetition of the same theme, at this point of our story it may be well to recall that the Daniel story stretched over four centuries. The last author to edit it lived during the days of persecution under Antiochus IV (167–164 B.C.). He stuck to the general theme: the encouragement of the persecuted Hebrews to resist Antiochus and the paganism he represented. Tradition from the Babylonian Captivity helped him to give examples of faith and courage under similar duress. By a series of tableaux — a peculiarly Hebrew style of emphasizing a point — the editor recounted the past and showed how relevant it was to the present. He led the reader to accept, though not necessarily to understand, Daniel's own bewildering dreams and visions. This was how he maintained unity in his writing.

Dreams and Visions

In the first of his dreams Daniel sees four sea monsters so fantastically ugly they beggar description. When you read about them, they seem more like nightmares than dreams. But all the four beasts symbolize the four kingdoms and their kings who caused the Israelites untold trouble. (The Apostle John used almost the same imagery in the Apocalypse to describe Roman persecutions.) I wonder if the editor is not taking some revenge upon the persecutors by depicting them so gruesome. The Little Horn especially, which can be taken as a nickname for Antiochus IV, gets his share of rough treatment: he has iron teeth and bronze claws, eyes, and a mouth that speaks arrogantly (cf. Dan 7:19–20). He is the king who makes war against God's people until the Ancient One (God) comes along and takes his power away. Then all kingship and dominion and majesty is handed over to the "son of man" (Christ), the familiar title by which the author suggests that the Messiah is both man and God.

Speaking in the first person, "I, Daniel," the writer gives a powerful account of the fight between a two-horned ram and a he-goat (three rival nations), and how after their horns are broken the Little Horn again emerges victorious. The angel Gabriel helps Daniel to interpret his vision, a vision referring to the end time in which the messianic era begins and ends. After such a vision, Daniel is "weak and ill for some days" (Dan 8:27).

The next vision has Daniel counting the number of years between the Babylonian exile and the persecution under Antiochus. He picks the number "seventy," which Jeremiah thought was the number of years the exile would last, and extends it to seventy weeks of years. Seventy weeks of years is seven times seventy or four hundred and ninety years. This is a round figure, only an approximation, but no matter how baffling the number is (it has confused biblical scholars for centuries), it is meant to span the years from 605 to 164 B.C. The last week of years (170–164 B.C.) marks the time of the persecution of Antiochus IV. And 160 years later the messianic era begins.

Desecration of the Temple

The last three and a half years of the persecution (167–164) are the most insufferable. During this Maccabean time

Antiochus desecrates the Jerusalem temple. It is not sure how he does it. Perhaps he initiates the horrible abomination, "the abomination of desolation," by setting up an altar and statue to the Olympian god Zeus, where swine flesh is offered up, or by dedicating the whole temple to him. His action is equivalent to destroying the temple. And that is why our Lord recalls this passage when predicting the ruin of the temple.

One of the more consoling events that Daniel envisions for the future is the resurrection of the dead. His is the first clear mention of it in the Old Testament. "Many of those who sleep in the dust of the earth shall awake; some shall live forever, others shall be an everlasting horror and disgrace" (Dan 12:2). Up to this moment the Hebrews had no indication of an afterlife. Contrast, if you will, such an outlook toward an unknown future — nothing certain beyond the grave — with our firm Christian belief that God will forever reward the good and punish the evil.

Of course Daniel has no view of a far-off future as we may have nowadays. He is looking to the immediate future when God's people will be freed from persecution. And yet we Christians, reflecting upon his words, seem to find in them hints of an everlasting future.

Again drawing upon his lively imagination, he pictures the names of the free written in a book, the book of life. "At that time your people shall escape, everyone who is found written in the book" (Dan 12:1). Daniel is not to reveal their names. "As for you, Daniel, keep secret the message and seal the book until the end of time; many shall fall away and evil shall increase" (Dan 12:4). Daniel himself is assured of a reward: "Go, take your rest, you shall rise for your reward at the end of days" (Dan 12:13).

An Appendix

With the guarantee of a lasting reward Daniel wants to

clinch his argument that faith in God must bear with persecution and hardship. The story of Susanna is told not merely to exemplify how wise Daniel is but to exhort the faithful to keep the law even at the risk of death. Susanna is willing to protect her chastity even if the false accusations brought against her by the two lecherous old fellows mean death for her. "O eternal God, you know what is hidden and are aware of all things before they come to be: you know that they have testified falsely against me. Here I am about to die, though I have done none of the things with which these wicked men have charged me" (Dan 13:42–43).

Daniel ends his story with a twofold experience which leads him again to the lions' den. This time he exposes the deceit of some priests who make their living by worshiping the idol called Bel (identical with the god Marduk). The idol supposedly eats all the food supplied by the duped worshipers. Daniel's detective work proves that in reality the priests and their families are entering the temple secretly and consuming all the food. Another idol the Babylonians are worshiping, a dragon, Daniel blows to bits with some homemade dynamite. All of this iconoclastic action brings condemnation on his head.

He is tossed to the lions again. This is the scene where Daniel sees the prophet Habakkuk carried by the crop of his hair. The angel deposits Habakkuk atop the den, and he lowers down a lunch for Daniel. The king arrives on the scene seven days later and finds Daniel sitting alive and peaceful. The king's words on this occasion not only express his own mind but sum up the whole theme of the Daniel story: "You are great, O Lord, the God of Daniel, and there is no other besides you!" (Dan 14:41). In a time of persecution and oppression, when faith is put to a severe test, no words are more comforting.

XV

John the Baptist

THE Church of Sancta Maria in Dominica in Rome boasts a majestic mosaic of John the Baptist. He is pictured standing and pointing to Christ. That gesture of his symbolizes his entire role in life. His duty is to introduce the Messiah, a role evidenced by the Gospels, each of which begins with John the Baptist (excepting the Infancy narrative). During the Advent liturgy, the Church, by select passages from the Gospels of Matthew, John, and Luke, features John the Baptist in his role of forerunner of the Messiah. As the Messiah is our forerunner to heaven, so is John the forerunner of the Messiah on earth.

The Birth of John

The precursor's birth was most extraordinary. It was the fruit of faith and prayer. His parents, Elizabeth and Zechariah, longed for a child, but they were already "advanced in years" (Lk 1:7). Knowing something of the Hebrew attitude toward childlessness — they considered it a curse — we can well imagine how Elizabeth and Zechariah felt about it. Have you ever

met the husband and wife who prayed long and hopefully
for a child to brighten their home? Then, unexpectedly, a
child is given to them. What a joy that child is to them! The
angel who announced John's birth predicted as much for his
parents: "And thou shalt have joy and gladness, and many
will rejoice at his birth. For he shall be great before the
Lord . . ." (Lk 1:14–15). Zechariah was unbelieving at first,
and for his lack of faith was struck dumb temporarily.

When Elizabeth was with child for six months, the good
news of her pregnancy was relayed to Mary. Mary came "with
haste" to visit Elizabeth, and their meeting was memorable.
As the gospel story has it, after Mary greeted Elizabeth, it was
not Elizabeth who first returned the greeting but the child
in her womb. For that meeting was not merely one between
Mary and Elizabeth but one more important between the
Messiah and his messenger John. John was so happy at this
first silent encounter that he leaped with joy. In a secret,
mysterious way the two recognized each other. Already the
child John announced the coming of the Messiah. And already the Messiah sent the Holy Spirit upon John and
cleansed him from original sin. A birthday gift to him.

The event of his birth gave everyone cause to marvel. Born
to parents who were past the childbearing age? When relatives and neighbors heard about the miraculous birth, they
rejoiced with them. But they were puzzled too that the child
should not be named after its father. They wondered why
the father should be dumb until the moment of the circumcision when he wrote "John is his name" on the writing
tablet. Everyone questioned himself, "What then will this
child be?" Certainly "the hand of the Lord was with him"
(Lk 1:66). Under divine inspiration Zechariah prophesied
the child's future to them, though they did not catch the
full meaning of his words. He will be "the prophet of the
Most High," and will "go before the face of the Lord to
prepare his ways" (Lk 1:76).

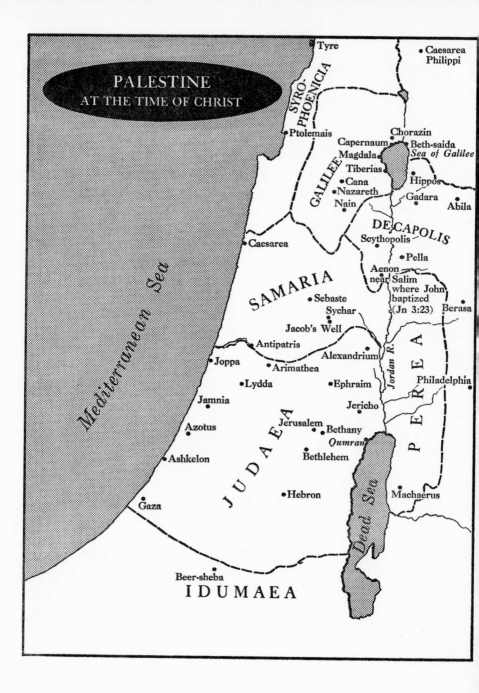

PALESTINE
AT THE TIME OF CHRIST

Tyre

Caesarea
Philippi

SYRO-
PHOENICIA

Ptolemais

GALILEE

Chorazin
Capernaum   Beth-saida
Magdala   *Sea of Galilee*
Tiberias
Cana   Hippos
Nazareth   Gadara
Nain   Abila

DECAPOLIS

Caesarea   Scythopolis

SAMARIA   Pella

                   Aenon
                   near Salim
                   where John
Sebaste   baptized
Sychar   (Jn 3:23)   Berasa
Jacob's Well

Antipatris
                   Alexandrium
Joppa
     Arimathea   PEREA
Lydda   Ephraim   Philadelphia

Jamnia   Jericho

Azotus   Jerusalem
            Bethany
Ashkelon   *Qumran*
            Bethlehem

Mediterranean Sea

JUDAEA

            Hebron   Machaerus

Gaza

                   Dead Sea

Beer-sheba
IDUMAEA

In the Desert

"And the child grew and became strong in spirit; and was in the deserts until the day of his manifestation to Israel" (Lk 1:80). John, in fact, was to spend most of his days in the desert — about thirty years in all. There he was — a gaunt figure, dressed coarsely in camel's hair with a leather girdle about his waist. For his food he took only locusts and wild honey, following mostly a vegetarian diet. Later Christ was to say to His stubborn countrymen, "John the Baptist came neither eating bread nor drinking wine, and you say, 'He has a devil'" (Lk 7:33).

For John the desert was a place of solitude and silence, where he could commune with God. In the desert his life was hidden with Christ in God. He was biding his time there, preparing himself in silence and prayer for the great introduction to and announcement of the Messiah. No doubt he wanted to be fully ready for the event, in anticipation of the day when he would really "make ready the way of the Lord," somewhat in fulfillment of Isaian prophecy.

But the desert is not only a place of solitary silence where, according to the prophet Hosea, God speaks to the heart (2:16), but a place of combat with the devil. God and the devil, each for his own reason, inhabit the desert. God silently draws the soul to himself (as he once drew his people through the desert into the Promised Land), the devil attempts silently and slyly to divert the soul away from God. We know how Jesus was led into the desert to be tempted by the devil. To realize what a man of prayer John was in the desert, we need only compare his years of sojourn with God in the desert with his short term of preaching. The comparison is about thirty to one. Before preaching a baptism of repentance he practiced it.

Witness to Christ

John stands at the crossroads of Old and New Testament

history. He is not a breach — some erroneously think the New Testament is a thing apart from the Old — but a bridge between the two. He has in him something of the Old and a bit of the New, concentrating in himself a whole past and a whole people awaiting the Messiah. This fact is shown by the title "prophet" which is his by right of his message: "the word of God came to John" (Lk 3:2). John still is a prophet according to the Old Testament pattern, an eschatological prophet who stands at the edge of the end time, which is already begun.

If there was a remnant of Israel looking forward to the Christ, John was the spokesman of that remnant. "This man came as a witness, to bear witness concerning the light, that all might believe through him. He was not himself the light, but was to bear witness to the light" (Jn 1:7–8). When the Hebrews asked him for his identity, John told them, "I am the voice of one crying in the desert, 'Make straight the way of the Lord,' as said Isaiah the prophet" (Jn 1:23).

Fearlessly, loudly, and clearly John proclaimed his message, the good news of salvation. As every prophet is the mouthpiece of God, and John was the divine spokesman, the voice of God had to be faithful to the divine message: "Repent, for the kingdom of heaven is at hand" (Mt 3:2). The principal theme of his message was the inauguration of a spiritual kingdom admitting members to it irrespective of any blood ties with the Hebrew nation.

The Hebrews who returned from the Babylonian exile had a strong penchant to trace their family lineage back through many generations. This was their way of striking up connections with the chosen people. John the Baptist criticized their proud and false trust in birth and genealogy. God, he said, could raise up children for Abraham out of stones (cf. Mt 3:9). It was an emphatic way of saying that God's chosen people are those who treasure divine grace above familial ties or national loyalty.

That was one reason why John took for a subordinate theme of his discourses a baptism of repentance accompanied by a remission of sins. For us the word "repent" need not ring true to its original meaning. For John and his listeners it meant a complete about-face. It meant a change of heart, of attitude, a change in one's way of thinking and acting. It marked the end of an old life and the beginning of a new. Man must be absorbed in God and not in the world and its vanity.

In John's audience there were the rich, the tax collectors, soldiers. "What then are we to do?" they asked him. He showed each group how they might put his words into practice. The rich must learn to share wealth, tax collectors and other officials should not go beyond their power, and soldiers ought to be content with their lot, be merciful and not take goods unjustly from an enemy. Translated into modern idiom, his point is that the rich and poor, powerful and weak, sick and healthy — all rightfully belong to God's human family.

Baptism in the Jordan

John reached the peak of his public career at the shores of the river Jordan. There he baptized no more noble personage than the Messiah himself. Their meeting was the occasion for John to be introduced to the family of the Trinity. God the Father spoke from the heavens, and the Holy Spirit, who once introduced John, lying within the silent, dark confines of his mother's womb, to the Son of God, now brought the two face to face. Was this truly the day of their manifestation to Israel? It was Jesus' epiphany too, for Jesus was manifestly one gifted with the Holy Spirit. John's whole life thereafter was to bear witness to the Son of God, to make Him known to Israel.

A Man of Character

That was why John was so forgetful of self, so ready to

serve Christ, so retiring, so willing to slip into the background. His character had depth, his personality was deep and hidden, yet it had a silent magnetism that drew crowds to hear his message and endeared disciples to him, among whom were his namesake, John the Evangelist, and Andrew. The people were wondering if he might not be the Christ. "Who art thou?" (Jn 1:19.) His disciples were reluctant to leave his company even though he pointed Christ out to them: "Behold the lamb of God!" (Jn 1:36.)

Christ Himself gave full credit to John, saying that "among those born of women there has not risen a greater than John the Baptist" (Mt 11:11). He was not a flimsy character, a reed shaken by the wind. He was not a soft character, a man clothed in soft garments. He was more than a prophet, he was the returned Elijah. Christ made this clear by telling the crowds, "And if you are willing to receive it, he is Elijah who was to come" (Mt 11:7). A forerunner of the Messiah and the Son of Man, he prepared the way for his disciples to accept Christ. One of his ways was to teach them how to pray and fast: "Lord," the Apostles once asked Christ, "teach us to pray, even as John also taught his disciples" (Lk 11:1). On another occasion the disciples of John were curious why Jesus did not have His disciples fast: "Why do we and the Pharisees often fast, whereas thy disciples do not fast?" (Mt 9:14.)

A man so close to God as John was, was bound to attract others to God by his contact with them and example. In fact, some of the people were wondering "whether perhaps he might be the Christ" (Lk 3:15) or Elijah (Jn 1:21). John was the first to reject such an idea, and he would have been keenly disappointed, had he lived long enough, to see some of his loyal followers band themselves together against Christ (cf. Acts 19:1-7; 18:24-25).

But a man of God, while appealing by his life and conduct to the good-hearted and good-willed, could at the same time arouse enmity and jealousy. John the Baptist had the courage to reprimand the ruler Herod for his public scandal, the adulterous union with his brother's wife. Herod, on the other hand, respected John, "knowing that he was a just and holy man" (Mk 6:20), but being called down in public was too much for him to take. It may be too that he felt John was a political upstart and a threat to his own position, for he knew about John's popularity and strong, winning personality. So for almost a year John was kept imprisoned at Machaerus, an old fortress.

Like his Master, John "came unto his own and his own received him not" (Jn 1:11). He preceded the Messiah and Son of Man not only in a prophetic role but in the role of a suffering Servant. "They did to him whatever they wished" (Mt 17:12). The end was in sight. Herodias, the adulterous woman, because John excoriated her publicly, was out for his blood. At a wild party, as her daughter Salome fascinated the king with her dancing, she demanded the head of John the Baptist on a platter. The king felt some regret but shamelessly could not retract his promise. Certainly this was a way out of a possible public revolt if John became a political threat to Herod. The prophet's blood was spilled; he met the same fate as so many of his predecessors in the prophetic ministry. The platter was brought into the banquet room.

The memory of John lingered long afterward in our Lord's mind. A careful reading of the Gospels will reveal how often our Lord brought up his name in conversation. No one knew better than He how willing and happy John was to give way to Him: "This my joy, therefore, is made full. He must increase, but I must decrease" (Jn 3:30). Here was a martyr in the full sense of the word — a witness to Christ.

Johannine Characteristics

If only we were able to meet the man John himself, live with him, hear him speak, and follow the gesture pointing to the Idol of his life. The other alternative is to watch carefully the gospel descriptions, brief though they are, of this great saint.

There is no reason why we cannot learn from him, or rather ask him to teach us, in a disciple spirit, his prayerful silence. His desert silence was not empty but filled with the presence of Yahweh. In the midst of a world mad with noise, is it possible under his guidance to catch moments of blissful, prayerful silence?

Perhaps no saint led so consistently a life rigorous and ascetic as that of John the Baptist. His was an about-face from the world — from family, native countryside, life itself. The mystery of the cross was anticipated in him.

To face up to an adulterous king and expose his crime took courage. John ran the risk of truth. In a day of easy compromise, when we are given a daily diet of lies, we can esteem a man who stood for the truth. He prepared for the Way which was the Truth, which ultimately gave him Life.

John is quoted, "One mightier than I is coming after me, the strap of whose sandals I am not worthy to stoop down and loose" (Mk 1:7). Yet the warmest recommendation ever given by Christ for anyone was for this humble man: "Amen I say to you, among those born of women there has not risen a greater than John the Baptist" (Mt 11:11).

A great man of God, the last forerunner of Christ.